The Blue Ribbon Cook Book

THE BLUE RIBBON
COOK BOOK

BEING

A SECOND PUBLICATION OF "ONE
HUNDRED TESTED RECEIPTS,"
TOGETHER WITH OTHERS
WHICH HAVE BEEN
TRIED AND FOUND
VALUABLE

BY
JENNIE C. BENEDICT

"Tis an ill cook that cannot lick his own fingers."
– SHAKESPEARE: *Romeo and Juliet.*

LOUISVILLE
JOHN P. MORTON & COMPANY
1904

COPYRIGHT
JENNIE C. BENEDICT
1904

ISBN: 978-1-6673-0721-3 paperback
ISBN: 978-1-6673-0722-0 hardcover

PREFACE.

In offering to the public the revised edition of my Cook Book, I do it at the earnest request of many who found my little book of "One Hundred Tested Receipts" to be helpful.

In this edition I have tried to embody the choicest and most acceptable of all my recipes. I have not only added many to those previously published, but have compiled this book with a view of giving valuable suggestions to the *young housekeepers,* as well as to the most experienced ones, combined with the simplest formulae for menus for convalescents and menus for luncheons and dinners, formal and informal.

Remembering the many who come inquiring what brand of flour we use; what fat for frying; what baking powder; what yeast; thè best market for meat, game, fish, etc., I have included in this a miniature Housekeepers' Directory, which may be found in the back of the book.

JENNIE C. BENEDICT.

CHAFING DISH RECIPES

FRIED OYSTERS.

FRICASSEED OYSTERS WITH MUSHROOMS.

LITTLE PIGS IN BLANKETS.

CHICKEN WITH ASPARAGUS.

ANY OF THE SAUCES.

CREAM CHICKEN.

CREAMED EGGS.

CREAMED CALF BRAINS.

CREAMED SWEETBREADS.

PARISIENNE POTATOES.

LOBSTER A LA NEWBURG.

OYSTERS A LA NEWBURG.

INDEX

MEATS

POULTRY AND GAME

VEGETABLES

ENTREES

SAUCES

SALADS

SALAD DRESSINGS

SANDWICHES

DESSERTS

CAKES

FILLINGS FOR CAKES

ICES

MISCELLANEOUS

SIMPLE DISHES FOR THE SICK

MY WORK AND HOW IT GREW.

FEELING a desire to prove what a woman can do in the business world without capital, and being confronted with the necessity of falling into rank in the marts of trade, I began, eleven years ago, 1893, to examine myself for the purpose of ascertaining whether or not I possessed a God-given talent; and if so, what it was.

I very soon developed a very decided taste for *cooking* — although latent up to that time — and now I know that my real knowledge of the art (for cooking is an art) was very limited.

My first step was to find a carpenter who was willing to build me a kitchen and pantry *on time* — for on time it must be, as I must earn the money with which to pay for it. This was soon accomplished. The kitchen and pantry were built in a primitive and very inexpensive way, and was furnished on the same terms and principles. I cheerfully began, with the help of my Sarah (who, by the way, is still with me to-day). I confined my work to making fruit cakes (by my own recipe, found in this book), and to my surprise, I had more orders than I could fill.

In *six months* I had paid for my kitchen. I then decided to make my work general, and sent out my first circular soliciting orders, from a cup of chocolate to furnishing and serving a large reception.

Then the principals of two of the large schools in the city, realizing the great advantage of having lunches properly prepared for the pupils, asked me to supply lunches daily for them — which I did for four years.

During those years I had worked early and late, giving up everything absolutely, and devoting my entire time to my *art.* By this time I had ceiled the walls of my little kitchen; put in water and gas, and secured a gas stove, made to order for my own special use. At this time gas stoves were just coming, into use, and in one of the large plumbing establishments I taught the use and advantage of

15

natural gas for cooking, making enough thereby to have natural gas piped into my own home, and gas and water both into my own kitchen.

So it may be seen how rapidly and successfully my work developed.

The Courier-Journal then offered me the Household department of that paper—which department I edited for some time. I then formed classes on the chafing dish and gave lessons in my own kitchen. Many members of these classes are the young housekeepers of to-day.

About this time the Pure Food Exhibition was held in Louisville. Mrs. Dearborn, the principal of the Boston Cooking School, who was giving demonstrations for them, being unable, owing to severe illness, to carry out her contract with them, I filled out the unexpired time for her. This opened the doors and *hearts* of the Boston Cooking School to me, and I entered the school the following winter, under the most favorable circumstances, and took a special course. There I found my inspiration for higher things, and learned each day what an art and science I had selected as my life work, and what great *possibilities* were held out to me in it.

Returning, I went to work in earnest, determined to strive for the topmost round of the ladder. Then it was, with fresh energy and determination, I broadened my work and taught cooking—not only at home, but in many points in my own State. Upon those classes I shall ever look back as among *the most delightful and refreshing experiences of my business career.*

In 1897, at the request of many for my recipes, I decided to publish my little book of "One Hundred Tested Receipts," but not until I had subscriptions enough to pay for the complete edition.

Two years later I was forced to give up my work temporarily, and in the fall of the same year, as chairman of the Lunch Committee, I took charge of and personally conducted the lunch room at the Business Woman's Club, which position I filled until April, 1900, when, with Miss S. E. Kerr, my present business associate, we bought out an established catering business on Fourth Street, where we now are fully equipped for any order, however large.

For those who would like to follow the same business, and there are many, for rarely a day passes that some one does not come in seeking suggestions and advice as to how to take up the work as I did — for the benefit of these, I will say it is not by any means smooth sailing; that there are many *snags* which might be emphasized. First of all, we *must* make sacrifices at every point, and social duties must be wholly abandoned. No business requires more tact, patience, or originality, and surely none requires closer attention or more constant study. One has to fully realize that she must think, plan, and entertain. She must be ready to suggest new menus, originate artistic table decorations, and *carry out* unique ideas in forms of entertainment, being ready with attractive souvenirs, keeping abreast and often *ahead* of the times.

She can not depend upon other people's books or ideas for new dishes or garnishings, but must be able to think them out for herself. Never be satisfied with anything but the purest and best material and the most skilled workmen. Without these two essentials we can not expect to make a success of the undertaking. We have found that cooking possesses the dignity of an art, of a science, and of a philosophy, and in its place in this age it is one of the still unseen powers that uplifts and enables our great people to progress.

"It is not the branch of work alone that lifts to a higher sphere,
For man may choose the humblest part, to find the great is near.
 God gives us all our part to do, and with our life the right
To leave our path unbeautified, or mighty in His sight."

JENNIE C. BENEDICT.

We quote the following interesting article from the Boston Cooking School Magazine:

LOVE FOR WORK.

Love of the work — contentment, as President Eliot puts it — is the key to the solution of the labor problem. By enthusiasm we overcome obstacles and reach the final goal. People are very likely to gain, at least in a measure, that which they most earnestly strive for. Difficulty after difficulty is overcome, and the object or end, long sought perhaps, is at last attained. The single eye, or desire to win, is the secret to all successful achievement. "The ideal man is a worker," or, as Carlyle tells us, "the captains of the world have been the leaders of industry."

On the contrary, nothing good can come out of dissatisfaction and discontent. We do best that which we are fond of doing, and a work well done always brings to the doer its own rich reward of pleasure and satisfaction.

Perhaps no kind of work is more wont to be irksome than that of housekeeping; and one reason for this is that it is done so poorly. The atmosphere of contentment is wanting. To remedy this, the kitchen in our homes should be thoughtfully planned and well equipped with the best-known appliances. The accessories and facilities for good work should be suitable and convenient. In a word, a kit of tools and proper materials are quite essential to good workmanship. Whereas too often the kitchen is the most ill-constructed and worst neglected part of the house, the aim being not so much to simplify processes as to cheapen them, not so much to secure the best results as to limit the cost of living. We must not forget the fact that good work of every class calls for generous outlay of both money and labor.

But, above all else, the zeal of the workman is best conducive to the highest ends. As a recent writer so well says: " Honest work springs from the heart. It can not be done without an intrinsic love for it. It is the honor and the love that are put into it that glorify the work. 'According to a law of worship, a devotee can never rise above the God he worships. So a man who devotes himself to art or to trade or the professions becomes identified with the principles embodied in the sciences and arts. If his work is done nobly, he becomes himself noble.' We must get rid of the false sentiment that grades different ranks of work as more or less respectable. It is cleanly and honest doing that gives rank to the task."

GLOSSARY.

SAUTE.—Saute is to fry in as little fat as possible—frying is to immerse in hot fat.

MARINATE.—To make salads successfully, the meat or celery or nuts should be placed in a dish and covered with three parts oil and one part vinegar, and a little salt, which is to marinate for several hours. Then any of the dressing which is not absorbed should be drained off, the salad mixed as desired, and the regular dressing poured over it.

BROWN STOCK.—To make brown stock successfully, take a four-pound soup bone, remove some of the meat from the bone, and then place the bone in the soup kettle with three quarts of cold water and let it boil on the back of the stove. Take the soup vegetables with a little parsley and two cloves and the meat which you have reserved from the soup bone, chop all fine and saute until brown. Pour into the boiling kettle and let all boil together slowly five or six hours. Remove from the fire, strain through a fine sieve, let it cool, and skim off the grease. Put away in a cool place and use as desired.

WHITE STOCK.—Take the liquor in which chicken or veal has been boiled, remove the meat and season, boil for fifteen minutes with a stalk of celery, a slice of onion, two slices of carrot and a bay leaf, and a little salt and pepper. Strain and use as white stock.

DILUTED EGG.—Where egg and crumbs are to be used in frying, always dilute one egg with two tablespoonfuls of water. This will prevent a hard crust from forming on anything that is fried, and will make just a delicate brown.

CAKE.—To obtain the best results in making cake where milk and baking powder are to be used, stir into the milk the baking powder and add to the cake the last thing, for in many cases, where the baking powder is put into the flour, some of it is lost, and the cake is not as light as it should be.

CAKE.—In plum puddings, fruit cakes, mince meat, etc., where spices and liquor are used, I find it more desirable to let the spices stand in the liquor for an hour or more before putting into the other ingredients.

WHIPPED CREAM. — Remember that a pint of cream whipped is not a pint of whipped cream. Be careful to notice always whether the recipe calls for whipped cream or cream whipped.

RICE. — It is a most satisfactory way to soak rice in cold water for an hour or more before using.

COOKING OF VEGETABLES. — A small scrubbing-brush, which may be bought for five cents, and two small pointed knives for preparing vegetables, should be found in every kitchen. Vegetables should be washed in cold water, and cooked until soft in boiling salted water; if cooked in an uncovered vessel, their color is better kept. For peas and beans add salt to water last half hour of cooking. Time for cooking the same vegetable varies according to freshness and age, therefore time-tables for cooking serve only as guides.

SOME flour requires more liquid to moisten than others, so your judgment must guide you in bread-making or pastry. Winter wheat flour requires less water than spring wheat flour.

IN SETTING bread to rise, be careful to place it where it is not too hot or too cool.

BE CAREFUL to save all trimmings of bread and all remnants of loaf bread to grind into crumbs for frying.

To TEST the temperature for frying, put Snowflake oil or lard in a saucepan and place on fire. When it begins to smoke, drop a piece of cold light bread in the fat, and if the bread browns at once, the fat is hot enough for frying.

THE most economical, and by all means the most desirable "fat" for frying purposes, is Snowflake oil.

WHERE a recipe calls for a cup of anything, always use the standard measuring cup.

IN BOILING chicken or sweetbreads put from one to three

tablespoons of lemon juice in water. This will blanch and make very tender.

To EXTRACT juice from onion, use an old onion; hold firmly in your hand and press the stem end firmly on a grater, pressing hard and turning just a little. Be careful not to grate.

To REMOVE the odor of onions from the hands, crush parsley in the fingers.

To SELECT A LOBSTER. — Take in the hand, and if heavy in proportion to its size, the lobster is fresh. Straighten the tail, and if it springs into place the lobster was alive

(as it should have been) when put into the pot for boiling. There is greater shrinkage in lobsters than in any other fish.

To OPEN LOBSTERS. — Take off large claws, small claws, and separate tail from body. Tail meat may sometimes be drawn out whole with a fork; more often it is necessary to cut the thin shell portion (using scissors or a can opener) in under part of the tail, then the tail meat may always be removed whole. Separate tail meat through center, and remove the small intestinal vein which runs its entire length; although generally darker than the meat, it is sometimes found of the same color. Hold body shell firmly in left hand, and with first two fingers and thumb of right hand draw out the body, leaving in shell the stomach (known as *the lady*), which is not edible, and also some of the green part, the *liver*. The liver may be removed by shaking the shell. The sides of the body are covered with the *lungs;* these are always discarded. Break body through the middle and separate body bones, picking out meat that lies between them, which is some of the sweetest and tenderest to be found. Separate large claws at joints. If shells are thin, with a knife cut off a strip down the sharp edge, so that shell may be broken apart and meat removed whole. Where shell is thick, it must be broken with a mallet or hammer. Small claws are used for garnishing. The shell of body, tail, and lower part of large claws, if not broken, may be washed, dried, and used for serving of lobster meat after it has been prepared. The portions of lobsters which are not edible are *lungs, stomach* (lady), and *intestinal vein. — Boston Cooking School Book.*

BREAD.

POTATO ROLLS.

1 cup flour.	1 cup potatoes (which have been
3/4 cup of lard.	put through a potato-ricer).
1 cup of milk.	2 eggs, well beaten.
1/2 cup of sugar (scant).	1 teaspoonful of salt.
1 cake of Fleischmann's Compressed Yeast, dissolved in 2 cups	
of lukewarm water.	

I cake of Fleischmann's Compressed Yeast, dissolved in 2 cups of lukewarm water.

Mix thoroughly the lard, potatoes, sugar, and salt; add the eggs, then the milk, and then the yeast. Set to rise for two hours; make into a soft dough by adding about a quart of flour, and set to rise again. Make into rolls or loaf, butter the top, and set to rise again; bake in a quick oven.

PLAIN ROLLS.

1 pint of milk.	2 tablespoonfuls of butter.
2 tablespoonfuls of sugar.	1 teaspoonful of salt.
3 cups of flour for sponge.	1/4 cup of lukewarm water.
1/4 cake of Fleischmann's Compressed Yeast.	

Scald the milk and pour it over the butter, sugar, and salt. When cold, add the yeast cake dissolved in the lukewarm water, then add the flour to make the sponge; beat well; let it rise until light. Then add enough flour to knead; knead well—very thoroughly—and set to rise. When light, cut it down, shape into rolls, let rise again, and bake in a quick oven.

PARKER HOUSE ROLLS.

2 cups scalded milk.	1 teaspoon salt.
3 tablespoons butter.	1 yeast cake dissolved in 1/4
2 tablespoons sugar.	cup lukewarm water.
	Flour.

Add butter, sugar, and salt to milk; when lukewarm, add dissolved yeast cake and three cups of flour. Beat thoroughly, cover, and let rise until light; cut down, and add enough flour to knead (it will take about two and one half cups). Let rise again, toss on slightly floured board, knead, pat, and roll out to one third inch thickness. Shape with biscuit-cutter, first dipped in flour. Dip the handle of a case knife in flour, and with it make a crease through the middle of each piece; brush over one half of each piece with melted butter, fold, and press edges together. Place in greased pan, one inch apart, cover, let rise, and bake in hot oven twelve to fifteen minutes. As rolls rise they will part slightly, and if hastened in rising are apt to lose their shape.

ENTIRE WHEAT BREAD.

2 cups scalded milk.	1 teaspoon salt.
1/4 cup sugar, or	1 yeast cake dissolved in
1/3 cup molasses.	1/4 cup lukewarm water.
4 2/3 cups coarse entire wheat flour.	

Add sweetening and salt to milk; cool, and when lukewarm add dissolved yeast cake and flour; beat well, cover, and let rise to double its bulk. Again beat, and turn into greased bread pans, having pans one half full; let rise, and bake. Entire wheat bread should not quite double its bulk during last rising. This mixture may be baked in Gem pans.

BAKING POWDER BISCUIT.

2 cups flour.	1 tablespoon lard.
4 tablespoons baking powder.	3/4 cup milk and water in
1 teaspoon salt.	equal parts.
1 tablespoon butter.	

Mix dry ingredients and sift twice.

Work in butter and lard with tips of fingers; add gradually the liquid, mixing with knife to a soft dough. It is impossible to determine the exact amount of liquid, owing to differences in flour. Toss on a floured board, pat, and roll lightly to one half inch in thickness. Shape with a biscuit-cutter. Place on buttered pan, and bake in hot oven twelve to fifteen minutes. If baked in too slow an oven, the gas will escape before it has done its work.

BEATEN BISCUIT.

1 quart of flour.	1/4 cup of lard.
1 cup of cold water.	1/2 teaspoonful of salt.

Add two tablespoonfuls of milk with the water (to make them brown nicely). Rub the lard well into the flour, and add the milky water until you have a stiff dough. Work through a biscuit machine, or beat with an iron until the dough is smooth and light. Bake in a moderate oven.

CORN MUFFINS.

1 pint of meal.	1/2 pint of milk.
1 tablespoonful of lard.	2 eggs.
1 heaping teaspoon baking powder.	1/2 teaspoon of salt.

Beat the eggs separately until very light. Then add to the yelks the meal, baking powder, and salt sifted together. Then the lard melted, then the milk, and when just ready to pour into the hot buttered rings, add the whites of eggs beaten to a stiff, dry froth.

WAFFLES.

2 cups of flour.	1 teaspoonful of baking powder (heaping).
1/2 teaspoonful of salt.	1 1/2 tablespoonfuls melted butter.
2 eggs, well beaten.	
1 cup milk.	

Mix the flour, baking powder and salt, and sift; then add the well-beaten yelks of two eggs, to which has been added the milk, and stir into the dry mixture. Add the melted butter, then the whites of the two eggs, beaten to a stiff froth. Then have the waffle irons very hot and well greased—pouring off any extra grease, leaving only enough to keep batter from sticking.

BUCKWHEAT CAKES.

1/3 cup fine bread crumbs or meal.   1/4 yeast cake.
2 cups scalded milk.   1/2 cup lukewarm water.
1/2 teaspoon salt.   1 3/4 cups buckwheat flour.
1 tablespoon molasses.

Pour milk over crumbs, and soak thirty minutes; add salt, yeast cake dissolved in lukewarm water, and buckwheat to make a batter thin enough to pour. Let rise over night; in the morning, stir well, add molasses, one fourth teaspoon soda dissolved in one fourth cup lukewarm water, and cook as griddle-cakes. Save enough batter to raise another mixing, instead of using yeast cake; it will require one half cup.

SOFT CORN BREAD (SPOON BREAD).

1 1/2 pints of sweet milk.   3/4 pint of meal.
1 egg.   Salt.
1 teaspoonful of quick yeast.

Bake in oven.

LUNCHEON ROLLS.

1/2 cup scalded milk.   2 tablespoons melted butter.
2 tablespoons sugar.   1 egg.
1/4 teaspoon salt.   Flour.
1/2 yeast cake dissolved in 2 tablespoons lukewarm water.

Add sugar and salt to milk; when lukewarm, add dissolved yeast cake and three fourths cup flour. Cover and let rise; then add butter, egg well beaten, and enough flour to knead. Let rise again, roll to one half inch thickness, shape with small biscuit-cutter, place in buttered pan close together, let rise again, and bake.

SOUR MILK GRIDDLE=CAKES.

2 1/2 cups flour.   2 cups sour milk.
1/2 teaspoon salt.   1 1/4 teaspoons soda.
1 egg.

Mix and sift flour, salt and soda; add sour milk, and egg well

25

beaten. Drop by spoonfuls on a greased hot griddle; cook on one side. When puffed, full of bubbles, and cooked on edges, turn, and cook other side. Serve with butter and maple syrup.

SWEET MILK GRIDDLE=CAKES.

3 cups flour.	1/4 cup sugar.
1 1/2 tablespoons baking powder.	2 cups milk.
1 teaspoon salt.	1 egg.

2 tablespoons melted butter.

Mix and sift dry ingredients; beat egg, add milk, and pour slowly on first mixture. Beat thoroughly, and add butter. Cook as Sour Milk Griddle Cakes.

SOUPS.

BROWN SOUP STOCK.

6 lbs. shin of beef.	1 sprig marjoram.
3 quarts cold water.	2 sprigs parsley.
1/2 teaspoon peppercorns.	Carrot,
6 cloves.	Turnip, } 1/2 cup each, cut in dice.
1/2 bay leaf.	Onion,
3 sprigs thyme.	Celery,
	1 tablespoon salt.

Wipe beef, and cut the lean meat in inch cubes. Brown one third of meat in hot frying-pan in marrow from a marrow bone. Put remaining two thirds with bone and fat in soup kettle, add water, and let stand for thirty minutes. Place on back of range, add browned meat, and heat gradually to boiling point. As scum rises it should be removed. Cover and cook slowly six hours, keeping below boiling point during cooking. Add vegetables and seasonings, cook one and one half hours, strain, and cool as quickly as possible.

JULIENNE SOUP.

To one quart clear brown soup stock add one fourth cup each carrot and turnip, cut in thin strips one and one half inches long, previously cooked in boiling salted water, and two tablespoons each cooked peas and string beans. Heat to boiling point.

CONSOMME.

2 lbs. lean beef (from the round).	1 small chicken.
2 ounces lean ham.	1 small onion.
2 sprigs parsley.	1/4 small carrot.
2 bay leaves.	2 stalks celery.
6 cloves.	2 eggs.
1/2 lemon (juice of same).	A little celery salt.

Wipe and cut the beef into small pieces; cut the chicken as for fricasseed chicken. Cover with cold water, and stand on the back of the stove where it will slowly heat. Simmer gently for four hours. Fry out a slice of bacon, add the ham cut in dice, the onion and carrot sliced, saute to a delicate brown in two tablespoonfuls of butter; then add this to the stock with the remainder of the vegetables (cutting the celery in pieces) and a little thyme. Let the soup simmer for another hour, strain and stand away to cool. When cold, carefully remove the fat from the surface; put in a kettle over the fire, add the whites and shells of two eggs beaten lightly, two tablespoons of cold water, a little celery salt, and the juice of half a lemon. Let it boil for five minutes, take from the fire and skim carefully, and strain through a cloth. When ready to serve, heat again and season with salt and pepper to taste. The soup should be perfectly clear, but amber in color.

QUICK BOUILLON.

1 tablespoon of butter.	1/2 small onion, sliced.
1 1/2 lbs. of lean chopped beef (round being best).	1 stalk of celery.
	1/2 chicken (bones well broken).
4 cloves.	2 slices carrot.
1 bay leaf.	2 sprigs of parsley.
1 1/2 pints cold water.	1 egg (white and shell).

Melt the butter and add the onion. Cook until the onion is thoroughly done, then add the beef (that from the round being best) and chicken, celery, cloves, carrot, bay leaf, parsley, and cold water. Cover the saucepan and set on the back of the stove where the water will slowly heat. Let it come to a boiling point, strain, and return to saucepan and bring to a boil. Beat the white of one egg in one half cup of water until thoroughly blended, crush the shell and add to the egg and water, and then to the boiling bouillon. Boil four minutes, let it stand one minute to settle, and strain through cheesecloth wrung out of cold water.

ICE BOUILLON.

Flavor bouillon with sherry or Maderia wine, and serve ice cold.

ST. GERMAIN.

1 can peas.	Water as much as there is liquor
1/2 onion.	in the can.
Sprig of parsley.	A blade of mace.
1/2 teaspoonful of sugar.	1 teaspoonful salt.
1/2 teaspoonful of pepper.	3 cupfuls brown stock.
	A bit of bay leaf.

Drain and mash the peas, add the water, reserving one half cup of the peas, putting the remainder into the stew pan with the onion, bay leaf, parsley, mace, sugar, salt, and pepper; simmer gently for half an hour, mash thoroughly, and add the hot brown stock. Let it come to the boiling point and rub through a sieve. Thicken with one tablespoonful of butter and one heaping tablespoonful of flour. Cook ten minutes and add the whole peas. — *Miss Farmer.*

CORN SOUP.

One half gallon of milk put on to boil. Cut one pint of green corn close to the ear, and put on with the milk; when it comes to a boil, add one pint of green com prepared as for pudding. Add butter as you would for oyster soup, salt and pepper to taste. Let boil until corn tastes done.

ASPARAGUS.

1 quart white stock.	1 can asparagus.
1 pint cream.	1 level tablespoon of butter.
	1 heaping teaspoonful flour.

Put a little more than a quart of white stock (either chicken or veal broth) on the fire with the asparagus, and let them boil hard for fifteen minutes, then strain, pressing all the substance from the asparagus—reserve the tips of asparagus to serve in puree. Thicken the strained stock with the butter and flour, and just before serving add the cream, salt, and pepper.

Celery, peas, etc., can be used in the same way.

WHITE SOUP.

1 chicken.	1/2 teaspoon salt.
6 blades of mace.	Little cayenne pepper.
8 almonds.	Yolks of 4 eggs.

1 quart of cream or milk.

Take one fat, old chicken and cut up; rub soup kettle with butter, put in chicken with one half teaspoon salt, little cayenne pepper, six blades of mace; cover well with water, stew slowly until done, skimming well, take breasts and wings, chop fine, steep remainder slowly, put three biscuits to soak in a cup of new milk, add yelks of four hard-boiled eggs, and chop fine eight almonds, pound chicken perfectly smooth, add soaked bread and eggs, little at a time, and pound to a smooth paste. Strain liquor from remaining chicken, which should be a full quart, pour by degrees into paste, stirring until well mixed; have boiling less than a quart of new milk or cream, add hot by degrees to the mixture, after which return the whole to the pot and let it simmer only a few minutes. Send to the table, and if not rich enough, add a small piece of butter. If the soup boils too much it will curdle. It should be as thick as rich cream.

SPLIT PEA SOUP.

1 cup dried split peas.	3 tablespoons butter.
2 1/2 quarts cold water.	2 tablespoons flour.
1 pint milk.	1 1/2 teaspoons salt.
1/2 onion.	1/8 teaspoon pepper.

2-inch cube fat salt pork.

Pick over peas and soak several hours, drain, add cold water, pork, and onion. Simmer three or four hours, or until soft; rub through a sieve. Add butter and flour cooked together, salt and pepper. Dilute with milk, adding more if necessary. The water in which a ham has been cooked may be used; in such case omit salt.

POTATO SOUP.

3 potatoes.	1 1/2 teaspoons salt.
1 quart milk.	1/4 teaspoon celery salt.
2 slices onion.	1/8 teaspoon pepper.
3 tablespoons butter.	Few grains cayenne.

2 tablespoons flour.   1 teaspoon chopped parsley.

Cook potatoes in boiling salted water; when soft, rub through a strainer. Scald milk with onion, remove onion, and add milk slowly to potatoes. Melt half the butter, add dry ingredients, stir until well mixed, then stir into boiling soup; cook one minute, strain, add remaining butter, and sprinkle with parsley.

OYSTER BISQUE.

1 quart of oysters.	4 cups of cream.
1 slice of onion.	2 stalks of celery.
2 blades of mace.	1 sprig of parsley.
A bit of bay leaf.	1/3 cup of butter.
1/3 cup of flour.	Salt and pepper to taste.

Scald the oysters and the liquor, separate them after heating to boiling point, strain liquor through cheesecloth, reheat, and thicken with the butter and flour. Scald the milk with the other ingredients mentioned, remove seasonings, add the milk to the oyster liquor, and then add the oysters. Serve hot with whipped cream on top.

TOMATO PUREE.

1 can tomatoes.	1 pint brown stock.
1 bay leaf.	1 sprig parsley.
1 stalk of celery.	1 teaspoonful of sugar.
1 tablespoonful of butter.	Several slices of onion.

Put the tomatoes into a saucepan with the brown stock, bay leaf, parsley, celery, and sugar; simmer thoroughly; put the onion and butter into the saute pan, and when the onion is thoroughly done—but not brown—add a tablespoonful of flour, and put all with the tomatoes; season with salt and pepper. Pass the whole through a fine sieve or strainer—heat again and serve.

CROUTONS (Duchess Crusts).

Cut stale bread in one third inch slices and remove crusts. Spread thinly with butter. Cut slices in one third inch cubes, put in pan and bake until delicately browned, or fry in deep fat.

NOODLES.

| 1 egg. | 1/2 teaspoon salt. | Flour. |

Beat eggs slightly, add salt, and flour enough to make very stiff dough; knead, toss on slightly floured board, and roll thinly as possible, which may be as thin as paper. Cover with towel, and set aside for twenty minutes; then cut in fancy shapes, using sharp knife or French vegetable cutter; or the thin sheet may be rolled like jelly-roll, cut in slices as thinly as possible, and pieces unrolled. Dry, and when needed cook twenty minutes in boiling salted water; drain, and add to soup.

Noodles may be served as a vegetable.

EGG BALLS.

| Yelks 2 hard-boiled eggs. | 1/3 teaspoon salt. |
| Few grains of cayenne. | 1/2 teaspoon butter. |

Rub yelks through sieve, add seasonings, and moisten with raw egg yelk to make consistency to handle. Shape in small balls, roll in flour, and saute in butter. Serve in brown soup stock, consomme, or mock turtle soup.

PÂTE À CHOUX.

2 1/2 tablespoons milk.	1/8 teaspoon salt.
1/2 teaspoon lard.	1/4 cup flour.
1/2 teaspoon butter.	1 egg.

Heat butter, lard, and milk to boiling point, add flour and salt, and stir vigorously. Remove from fire, add egg unbeaten, and stir until well mixed. Cool, and drop small pieces from tip of teaspoon into deep fat. Fry until brown and crisp, and drain on brown paper.

CRACKERS WITH CHEESE.

Arrange zephyrettes or saltines in pan. Sprinkle with grated cheese and bake until cheese is melted.

QUENELLES.

Quenelles are made from any kind of force-meat, shaped in small balls or between tablespoons, making an oval, or by forcing mixture through pastry bag on buttered paper. They are cooked in boiling salted water or stock, and are served as garnish to soups or other dishes; when served with sauce, they are an entrée.

FISH.

_____

FRIED OYSTERS.

Take large select oysters, wash and drain and wipe. Dip them in the yellow of an egg, diluted with two tablespoonfuls of water, then in bread or cracker crumbs; put in frying basket and fry in deep hot lard.

OYSTERS EN COQUILLE.

2 sets of calf brains.	50 oysters.

Carefully clean the brains and boil in salt water; scald the oysters in their own liquor until the edges curl, and then cut in small pieces. Chop the brains and mix with the oysters. Take two tablespoonfuls of butter and saute a little finely chopped onion in it; add to the brains and oysters a little chopped parsley, celery salt, salt and pepper. Then add one half cup of cream, two tablespoonfuls of stale bread crumbs.

FRICASSEED OYSTERS WITH MUSHROOMS.

Thirty oysters, one half cup sliced mushrooms, one tablespoonful butter, one tablespoonful of flour, three gills of cream, one gill of mushroom liquor, yelks of two eggs, season with salt, pepper, and a little celery salt. Cook together butter and flour over hot water, add seasoning, cream, and mushroom liquor, and then the egg very slowly, or it will curdle. Add oysters and mushrooms, and when the oysters are plump and edges curled, serve at once.

OYSTER RAREBIT.

6 oysters.	1/2 lb. of cheese.
2 eggs.	Salt spoon of salt.
1 tablespoon butter.	Salt spoon of mustard.
Salt spoon of cayenne pepper.	

Clean and remove the muscle from one half pint of oysters.

Parboil them in a chafing dish in their own liquor until the edges curl. Remove to a hot bowl. Put one tablespoonful of butter, one half pound of cheese, broken in small pieces, one salt spoon each of salt, mustard, and a few grains of cayenne pepper into the chafing dish. While the cheese is melting beat two eggs slightly and add to them the oyster liquor. Mix this gradually with the melted cheese, add the oysters, and turn out and serve over hot toast.

OYSTERS A LA NEWBURG.

25 oysters.	Salt spoon of salt.
Heaping tablespoon butter.	Yelk of 1 egg.
1/2 salt spoon of pepper.	4 spoons of milk or cream.
2 teaspoons of sherry.	

Into a pan which is very hot throw your oysters, first having drained all the liquor from them. To twenty-five oysters allow a piece of butter the size of a walnut, pepper and salt. Stir until your oysters curl. Then quickly add the beaten yelk of an egg, to which has been added the milk or cream. After these are thoroughly mixed, add two teaspoonfuls of sherry; stir well, but do not allow the mixture to come to a boil. Serve on squares of toast.

OYSTER COCKTAIL.

Put six tablespoons of tomato catsup, three tablespo ns of Tarragon vinegar, three teaspoons of Worcestershire sauce, three drops of tobasco, eight small oysters in each glass, and on top of all sprinkle a teaspoonful of very finely chopped celery.

BROILED LIVE LOBSTER.

Live lobsters may be dressed for broiling at market, or may be done at home. Clean lobster and place in a buttered wire broiler. Broil eight minutes on flesh side, turn and broil six minutes on shell side. Serve with melted butter. Lobsters taste nearly the same when placed in dripping pan and baked fifteen minutes in hot oven, and are much easier cooked.

TO SPLIT A LIVE LOBSTER.

Cross large claws and hold firmly with left hand. With sharp-pointed knife, held in right hand, begin at the mouth and make a deep incision, and, with a sharp cut, draw the knife quickly through body and entire length of tail. Open lobster, remove intestinal vein, liver, and stomach, and crack claw shells with a mallet.

SALPICON OF LOBSTER.

Put one level tablespoon of butter in double boiler. Add one tablespoon of flour, then one quarter cup of cream, and one quarter cup of white stock; season with salt and cayenne, and when it thickens, add one tablespoon of chopped lobster, six mushrooms chopped fine, and one small truffle chopped fine. Serve in lobster claws or shells.

STUFFED LOBSTER.

Two pounds of lobster, one and one half cups of cream and rich white stock, bit of bay leaf, three tablespoons of butter, three tablespoons of flour, yelks of two eggs, one teaspoon of lemon juice, one teaspoon of chopped parsley. Season with salt, cayenne, and a little grated nutmeg. Scald stock with bay leaf and remove bay leaf. Melt butter, add flour, then stock and seasonings, then yelks slightly beaten, and the lemon juice. When sauce is thick, add lobster and fill the shell. Cover with buttered bread crumbs and brown. Serve in a nest of water cresses.

LOBSTER CUTLETS.

Melt two level tablespoonfuls of butter, add two heaping tablespoonfuls of flour, one teaspoonful of salt, pepper to taste, one half cup of white stock, and one half cup of cream. When smooth add one half teaspoon finely chopped parsley, one beaten egg, and enough chopped lobster, mushrooms, and truffles to make one pint. Cook a few minutes and pour out on platter, and let it get thoroughly cold (the colder the better). Shape, dip in bread crumbs, then egg, and then crumbs, and fry in hot fat.

LOBSTER TIMBALS.

2 slices of stale bread.	1 pound halibut or cod.
1 egg, 1 yelk.	4 tablespoonfuls of rich cream.
1/2 tablespoon onion chopped fine.	3 tablespoonfuls of butter.
2 tablespoonfuls of flour.	1 tablespoon sherry wine.
2/3 cup of lobster.	Salt and pepper to taste.

Soak two slices of stale bread in water until soft, squeeze until entirely free from water, cook with a teaspoonful of butter, beating to the consistency of India rubber, then cool; put one pound of halibut or cod through a meat chopper, and then pound in a mortar. Add gradually one third cup of bread, one egg, one yelk, and four tablespoonfuls of rich cream; beat well. Butter timbal molds and spread the bread mixture on sides and bottom ; fill with the following lobster filling:

Saute one half tablespoonful of onion, chopped very fine, in three tablespoonfuls of butter; add two tablespoonfuls of flour, one half cup of rich cream, yelks of two eggs, salt and pepper to taste. When this thickens, add a tablespoonful of sherry wine and two thirds of a cup of chopped lobster; pour out to cool, fill the center of the timbals, cover with the fish, and cook in a hot oven in a pan of hot water; serve with lobster sauce. This proportion makes six timbals.

LOBSTER A LA NEWBURG.

1 pint finely chopped lobster.	1/2 pint cream.
Yelks of 3 eggs.	1/3 glass of sherry.
1/2 teaspoonful of salt.	A little red pepper.

Put the cream, wine, and beaten yelks together in a double boiler and cook, stirring steadily until the sauce thickens. Put in the lobster, let it become heated through, season and serve. A larger portion of sherry may be used if desired. Be very careful to cook this over boiling water, as it curdles very easily.

TOMATOES STUFFED WITH LOBSTER OR FISH.

6 large ripe tomatoes.	1 cup of cream.
1 cup heaping full of lobster or fish.	1/2 teaspoon salt.
2 tablespoons of butter.	Few grains of pepper.
2 tablespoons of flour.	1 teaspoon lemon juice.

Melt the butter; add flour, and when thoroughly blended add the cream and seasonings. Cook until thick; then add the lobster meat or fish which has been cooked previously. Without peeling the tomatoes scoop out the tops and fill with creamed fish or lobster. Put in hot oven, and cook until tomatoes are thoroughly done. Then serve with allemande, bechamel, or mushroom sauce.

SOFT=SHELL CRABS.

Clean crabs, sprinkle with salt and pepper, dip in crumbs, egg, and crumbs, fry in deep fat, and drain. Being light, they will rise to top of fat, and should be turned while frying.

TO CLEAN A CRAB.

Lift and fold back the tapering points which are found on each side of the back shell, and remove spongy substance that lies under them. Turn crab on its back, and with a pointed knife remove the small piece at lower part of shell, which terminates in a point: this is called the apron.

TO BROIL A CRAB (SOFT SHELL).

Clean crab, sprinkle with salt and pepper, dredge with flour, and broil in butter. Garnish with water cress and lemon, and serve with or without tartar sauce.

TARTAR SAUCE.

One half cup of mayonnaise dressing (No. 1) ; add one teaspoon onion juice, a dessertspoon chopped capers, one teaspoon chopped pickle.

DEVILED CRABS (Hard Shell).

2 dozen crabs.	1/2 teaspoon mustard.
1 egg.	1 teaspoon thyme.
1/2 teaspoon salt.	Ground cloves, allspice, and
Little black or red pepper.	parsley.
1 level tablespoon butter.	1 tablespoon olive oil.
1 teaspoon of chopped onions.	

Boil two dozen crabs twenty minutes with a little salt, then remove meat, reserving the number of empty shells needed. The meat from two dozen crabs will fill nine shells. Cut the crab meat fine, mix it well with one raw (beaten) egg and the pepper, mustard, cloves, allspice, parsley, and thyme; add the olive oil, butter, and chopped onion. Let all stand a short time in a bowl until the meat is seasoned, stuff the empty shells, place them in a pan for baking, cover them with another raw beaten egg, mix with fine salted bread crumbs; bake in oven about fifteen minutes.

TO BROIL FISH.

Clean and wipe fish dry as possible, sprinkle with salt and pepper, and place in a well-greased wire broiler. Slices of fish should be turned often while broiling. Pompano, blue fish, and mackerel are split down the back and broiled whole, removing tail and head or not, as desired. Whole fish should be first broiled on flesh side and then turned and broiled on skin side, just long enough to make skin brown and crisp. To broil sliced fish, such as salmon, halibut, white fish, or trout, cut in two inch slices, and should be turned often while broiling.

BAKED RED SNAPPER.

Clean a four-pound red snapper, sprinkle the inside with salt and pepper, and stuff and sew together or pin together. Place in a greased pan, and if you have no fish sheet, fold in cheesecloth, bake in hot oven for about three quarters of an hour or until thoroughly done, basting frequently. Serve with hollandaise sauce or plain white sauce.

STUFFING FOR FISH.

1/2 cup cracker crumbs.
1/2 cup stale bread crumbs.
1/4 cup melted butter.
1/2 teaspoon salt.
1/8 tablespoon pepper.
1/2 cup of hot water.
Few drops of onion juice.

Mix ingredients in order given.

TO COOK FISH IN BOILING WATER.

Small cod, haddock, or cusk are cooked whole in enough boiling water to cover, to which is added salt and lemon juice or vinegar. Salt gives flavor; lemon juice or vinegar keeps the flesh white. A long fish-kettle containing a rack on which to place fish is useful but rather expensive. In place of fish-kettle, if the fish is not too large to be coiled in it, a frying-basket may be used placed in any kettle. The fish is cooked when flesh leaves the bone, no matter how long the time.

FISH PUDDING. **

1 pound boiled fish.
1 1/2 tablespoons of flour.
1/4 teaspoonful of pepper.
A little onion juice.
1/2 cup of cream.
1 1/2 teaspoons of salt.
1 teaspoonful lemon juice.
2 eggs.

Mash the fish thoroughly, then put through a puree sieve and add seasonings. Put butter in the saucepan, and when melted add the flour, then the cream, then the beaten eggs, stirring until well scalded, not thick. Then add the fish, beat well and fill a ring mold with the pudding, pressing it well against the sides; set the whole in a pan of water and put in a moderate oven for thirty minutes. Remove on to a dish, and fill in the center with Parisienne potatoes, making a border of the same outside, and serve with rich cream sauce, in which parsley is chopped. — *Century Cook Book.*

---

* If a dry fish, such as halibut or haddock, is used, slash body at intervals and insert thin slices of fat pork; in other words, lard it.

FISH CROQUETTES.

1 pint boiled fish.	1/2 teaspoonful of onion juice.
1/2 teaspoonful pepper.	1 tablespoonful of butter.
1 cupful of cream.	Yelks of two eggs and a little
2 tablespoonfuls of flour.	chopped parsley.

1 teaspoonful salt.

Put the butter into a saucepan; when melted add the flour, and when thoroughly mixed add the cream, then the seasonings, then the beaten yelks of two eggs, and then the fish and the parsley. Spread on a dish to cool; make out into croquettes; to the beaten yelk of one egg add two tablespoonfuls of water. Dip the croquettes first into the stale bread crumbs, then in egg, and then in crumbs. Fry in boiling fat. Serve with either bechamel or hollandaise sauce.

BROILED SHAD ROE.

Wash and dry the roe, then broil them very slowly and keep them moistened with butter to prevent the skin from breaking. They may also be cooked by sauteing in butter. Cook them brown, cover the top with butter, pepper, salt, and a little lemon juice, and sprinkle with chopped parsley. Garnish with lemon and water cress, and serve some of the water cress with each portion. Serve with maitre de hotel butter.

MEATS.

ROAST FILLET.

The fillet should be plentifully larded and all of the sinewy skin and gristle removed from the top, and most of the fat from the under side. Then place in a baking pan thin slices of larding or pickled pork, chopped onion, carrot, turnip, and celery; then place the fillet on this. Pour over it a cupful of brown stock, salt and pepper, chopped parsley, bay leaf, and cloves. Cook in a hot oven for thirty minutes, basting frequently. When done, drain off the gravy and remove grease from the top. Take a tablespoonful of butter, add a tablespoonful of flour, cook together until they are brown. Add the gravy and a little brown stock—a cupful in all—stir until it boils, add a canful of mushrooms, chopped, and let it simmer for five minutes; then add a little Madeira or sherry; pour round the fillet and serve.

BROILED FILLETS.

Select small beef tenderloins, two inches thick; lard thoroughly; let them lay for two hours in a strong, highly seasoned stock with two tablespoonfuls of claret; broil for a few minutes over a hot fire ; serve with drawn butter or mushroom sauce.

BROILED BEEFSTEAK.

Select porterhouse steak at least one inch thick. Wipe off with wet cloth, rub over with lemon. With some of the fat which must be trimmed off, grease wire broiler, and place meat in it. Broil over hot fire at first, that surface may be well seared, thus preventing escape of juices. After this, turn occasionally until well cooked on both sides. Remove to hot platter, spread with butter and sprinkle with salt and pepper.

BEEFSTEAK IN OYSTER BLANKET.

Select a porterhouse steak at least an inch and a half thick, remove the bone, wipe off with a wet cloth, rub over with lemon. With some of the fat which must be trimmed off, grease the wire broiler and place the meat in it; broil over a very hot fire at first that the surface may be well seared, thus preventing the escape of juices. After this, turn occasionally until cooked on both sides; remove to a baking pan, cover thoroughly with select oysters, placing a little butter here and there all over it. Squeeze the juice of half a lemon and place in a hot oven; cook until the oysters plump and the edges curl; season with salt and pepper. Serve with melted butter, a little lemon juice, and chopped parsley.

HAMBURG STEAKS.

Chop finely one pound lean raw beef; season highly with salt, pepper, and a few drops onion juice or one half shallot finely chopped. Shape, cook, and serve as meat cakes. A few gratings of nutmeg and one egg slightly beaten may be added.

LAMB CHOPS A LA MAINTENON.

Wipe six French chops, which should be one and one half inches thick. Split meat in half, cutting to the bone. Cook two and one half tablespoons of butter and one tablespoon of chopped onion five minutes, remove onion, add one half cup chopped mushrooms and cook five minutes. Add two tablespoons of flour, three tablespoons of brown stock, one teaspoon of finely chopped parsley, and season with salt and pepper. Spread this mixture between the split chops, press the edges well together, and broil eight minutes. Serve with melted butter or Spanish sauce.

MINCED LAMB ON TOAST.

Remove dry pieces of skin and gristle from remnants of cold roast lamb, then chop meat. Heat in well buttered frying-pan, season with salt, pepper, and celery salt, and moisten with a little hot water or stock; or, after seasoning, dredge well with flour, stir, and add enough stock to make thin gravy. Pour over small slices of buttered toast.

BREADED VEAL CUTLETS.

Leave the cutlet whole, or cut it into pieces of uniform size and shape. Salt and pepper. Dip in egg and cover with bread crumbs or cracker crumbs. Fry in hot lard and serve with tomato or cream sauce.

SCALLOPED LAMB.

Remove skin and fat from thin slices of cold roast lamb and sprinkle with salt and pepper. Cover bottom of baking dish with butter and cracker crumbs, cover crumbs with meat; cover meat with boiled macaroni and

add another layer of meat and macaroni; pour over tomato sauce and cover with buttered cracker crumbs. Bake in hot oven until crumbs are brown. Cold boiled rice may be used in place of the macaroni.

RAGÔUT OF VEAL.

Reheat two cups cold roast veal, cut in cubes, in one and one half cups brown sauce seasoned with one teaspoon Worcestershire sauce, few drops of onion juice, and a few grains of cayenne.

POULTRY AND GAME.

BROILED CHICKEN.

After chicken has been cleaned thoroughly, split through the back and wash and wipe well. Put a piece of bacon under each wing and on the broiler, and season well with salt, pepper, and butter. Broil twenty minutes over a clear fire, watching carefully and turning broiler so that all parts may be equally browned. The flesh side must be exposed to the fire the greater part of time, as the skin side will brown quickly. Remove to a hot platter, spread with soft butter, and sprinkle with salt and pepper. Chickens are so apt to burn while broiling that many prefer to partially cook in oven. Place chicken in dripping-pan, skin side down, sprinkle with salt and pepper, dot over with butter, and bake fifteen minutes in hot oven; then broil to finish cooking. Put on hot platter and garnish with pastry crullers and parsley.

CHICKEN GUMBO.

Dress, clean, and cut up a chicken. Sprinkle with salt and pepper, dredge with flour, and saute in pork fat. Fry one half finely chopped onion in fat remaining in frying pan. Add four cups sliced okra, sprig of parsley, and one fourth red pepper finely chopped, and cook slowly fifteen minutes. Add to chicken, with one and one half cups tomatoes, three cups boiling water, and one and one half teaspoons salt. Cook slowly until chicken is tender, then add one cup boiled rice.

ROAST TURKEY.

Dress, clean, stuff, and truss a ten-pound turkey. Place on its side on rack in a dripping-pan, rub entire surface with salt, and spread breast, legs, and wings with one third cup butter, rubbed until creamy and mixed with one fourth cup flour. Dredge bottom of pan with flour. Place in a hot oven, and when flour on turkey begins to

45

brown, reduce heat, baste with fat in pan, and add two cups boiling water. Continue basting every fifteen minutes until turkey is cooked, which will require about three hours. For basting, use one half cup of butter melted in one half cup boiling water, and after this is used baste with fat in pan. During cooking turn turkey frequently, that it may brown evenly. If turkey is browning too fast, cover with buttered paper to prevent burning. Remove string and skewers before serving. Garnish with parsley or celery tips.

For stuffing, use double the quantities given in recipes under Roast Chicken. If stuffing is to be served cold, add one beaten egg. Turkey is often roasted with chestnut stuffing.

GRAVY.

Pour off liquid in pan in which turkey has been roasted. From liquid skim off six tablespoons fat ; return fat to pan and brown with six tablespoons flour; pour on gradually three cups stock in which giblets, neck, and tips of wings have been cooked, or use liquor left in pan. Cook five minutes, season with salt and pepper; strain. For giblet gravy, add to the above, giblets (heart, liver, and gizzard) finely chopped.

CHESTNUT STUFFING.

3 cups French chestnuts.	1/8 teaspoon pepper.
1/2 cup butter.	1/4 cup cream.
1 teaspoon salt.	1 cup cracker crumbs.

Shell and blanch chestnuts. Cook in boiling salted water until soft. Drain and mash, using a potato ricer. Add one half the butter, salt, pepper, and cream. Melt remaining butter, mix with cracker crumbs, then combine mixtures.

MOCK TERRAPIN.

1 1/2 cups cold cooked chicken or veal cut in dice.	Whites 2 hard-boiled eggs, chopped.
1 cup White Sauce I.	3 tablespoons sherry wine.
Yelks 2 hard-boiled eggs finely chopped.	1/4 teaspoon salt.
	Few grains cayenne.

Add to sauce, chicken, yelks and whites of eggs, salt, and cayenne; cook two minutes, and add wine.

BROILED QUAIL.

Broil same as chicken. Allow eight minutes for cooking. Serve on toast and garnish with parsley and thin slices of lemon.

ROAST QUAIL.

Dress, clean, and stuff the same as chicken, adding pecans or oysters to dressing. Bind with thin slices of bacon and roast from fifteen to twenty minutes and serve with gravy.

GOOD STUFFING FOR TURKEY OR CHICKEN.

Moisten a cupful of bread crumbs with melted butter, season highly with salt, pepper, thyme, chopped parsley, and onion juice. Or, put in a saucepan a tablespoonful

of butter and fry in it one onion chopped fine, then add a cupful of bread which has been soaked in water, all of the water having been pressed out thoroughly, one half cupful of stock, a teaspoonful of salt, a teaspoon each of pepper and thyme, one half cup of celery cut into very small pieces. Stir it until it leaves the sides of the pan, then stuff either turkey or chicken. — *Century Cook Book.*

VEGETABLES.

BOILED POTATOES.

Select potatoes of uniform size. Wash, pare, and drop at once in cold water to prevent discoloration; soak one half hour in the fall, and one to two hours in winter and spring. Cook in boiling salted water until soft, which is easily determined by piercing with a skewer. For seven potatoes allow one tablespoon salt, and boiling water to cover. Drain from water, and keep uncovered in warm place until serving time. Avoid sending to table in a covered vegetable dish. In boiling large potatoes, it often happens that outside is soft, while center is underdone. To finish cooking without potatoes breaking apart, add one pint cold water, which drives heat to center, thus accomplishing the cooking.

MASHED POTATOES.

To five riced potatoes add three tablespoons butter, one teaspoon salt, few grains pepper, and one third cup hot milk; beat with fork until creamy, reheat, and pile lightly in hot dish.

DUCHESS POTATOES.

To two cups hot riced potatoes add two tablespoons butter, one half teaspoon salt, and yelks of three eggs slightly beaten. Shape (using pastry bag and tube) in form of baskets, pyramids, crowns, leaves, roses, etc. Brush over with beaten egg diluted with one teaspoon water, and brown in a hot oven.

POTATOES EN SURPRISE.

Season one pint of hot mashed potatoes with one tablespoonful of butter, one teaspoonful of salt, one fourth teaspoonful of celery salt, one fourth teaspoonful of pepper, and a few grains of cayenne.

Add six drops of onion juice, cool slightly, and add the yelk of one egg beaten slightly. Shape into balls. Make a hole in the center, fill with creamed chicken, oysters, or sweatbreads. Close up, dip in crumbs, diluted egg and crumbs, and place in a fryingbasket and fry in hot fat. Serve with cream or oyster sauce.

POTATO CROQUETTES.

2 cups hot riced potatoes.	1/4 teaspoon celery salt.
2 tablespoons butter.	Few grains cayenne.
1/2 teaspoon salt.	Few drops onion juice.
1/8 teaspoon pepper.	Yelk 1 egg.
1 teaspoon finely chopped parsley	

Mix ingredients in order given, and beat thoroughly. Shape, dip in crumbs, egg, and crumbs again, fry one minute in deep fat, and drain on brown paper. Croquettes are shaped in a variety of forms. The most common way is to first form a smooth ball by rolling one rounding tablespoon mixture between hands. Then roll on a board until of desired length, and flatten ends.

FRENCH FRIED POTATOES.

Wash and pare small potatoes, cut in eighths, lengthwise, and soak one hour in cold water. Take from water, dry between towels, and fry in deep fat. Drain on brown paper and sprinkle with salt. Care must be taken that fat is not too hot, as potatoes must be cooked as well as browned.

HASHED BROWN POTATOES.

Try out fat salt pork cut in small cubes; remove scraps; there should be about one third cup of fat. Add two cups cold boiled potatoes finely chopped, one eighth teaspoon pepper, and salt if needed. Mix potatoes thoroughly with fat; cook three minutes, stirring constantly; let stand to brown underneath. Fold as an omelet and turn on hot platter.

PARISIENNE POTATOES.

With a French vegetable cutter, cut potato balls out of peeled raw potatoes. Drop in cold water for about half an hour. Put into boiling salted water and boil about fifteen minutes or until tender. Drain off the water and let stand on the back of range, covered over, until dry. Serve with white sauce and chopped parsley.

STUFFED SWEET POTATOES.

Select good, firm sweet potatoes. Wash well and boil until tender, remove from fire, cut in half, take out most of the potato, leaving the skin firm enough to stuff. Mash potato well, season with butter, cream, a little sugar, and cinnamon and sherry wine to taste. Fill shells with potatoes and put in oven to brown a little.

GLAZED SWEET POTATOES.

Wash and pare six medium-sized potatoes. Cook ten minutes in boiling salted water. Drain, cut in halves lengthwise, and put in a buttered pan. Make a syrup by boiling three minutes one half cup sugar and four tablespoons water; add one tablespoon butter. Brush potatoes with syrup and bake fifteen minutes, basting twice with remaining syrup.

SWEET POTATOES EN BROCHETTE.

Wash and pare potatoes, and cut in one third inch slices. Arrange on skewers in groups of three or four, parboil six minutes, and drain. Brush over with melted butter, sprinkle with brown sugar, and bake in a hot oven until well browned.

SWEET POTATO CROQUETTES.

To two cups hot riced sweet potatoes add three table- spoons butter, one half teaspoon salt, few grains pepper, and one beaten egg. Shape in croquettes, dip in crumbs, egg, and crumbs again, fry in deep fat, and drain. If potatoes are very dry, it will be necessary to add hot milk to moisten.

BROILED TOMATOES.

Wipe and cut in halves crosswise, cut off a thin slice from rounding part of each half. Sprinkle with salt and pepper, dip in crumbs, place in a well-buttered broiler, and broil six to eight minutes.

STUFFED TOMATOES.

Take fine, large tomatoes, not too ripe. Cut out the blossom end and scoop out the inside as clean as you can without breaking the skins. Chop fine and add equal parts of ground chicken, green corn (uncooked), okra, and a few bread crumbs. Season well with salt and pepper and a very little onion juice. Fill skins, put a piece of butter on top of each, and place in a baking dish (buttered) and bake in a good oven.

BRUSSELS SPROUTS IN WHITE SAUCE.

Pick over, remove wilted leaves, and soak in cold water fifteen minutes. Cook in boiling salted water twenty minutes, or until easily pierced with a skewer. Drain, and to each pint add one cup white sauce.

BOILED CUCUMBERS.

Old cucumbers may be pared, cut in pieces, cooked until soft in boiling salted water, drained, mashed, and seasoned with butter, salt, and pepper.

FRIED CUCUMBERS.

Pare cucumbers and cut lengthwise in one third inch slices. Dry between towels, sprinkle with salt and pepper, dip in crumbs, egg, and crumbs again, fry in deep fat, and drain.

EGG PLANT A LA CREOLE.

Boil whole in salt water until done, but not over done. Cut in half and scoop out the meat, leaving enough in skin to form a shell. Mash the meat of egg plant, salt and pepper to taste, add the juice of a small onion, three fourths of a pint of toasted bread crumbs. Soften with a little milk, and add a can of dry shrimp chopped fine. Put back in shells with crumbs sprinkled on the top. Place a lump of butter the size of a walnut on each shell and slip in oven until a light brown.

STUFFED EGG PLANT.

Cook egg plant fifteen minutes in boiling salted water to cover. Cut a slice from top, and with a spoon remove pulp, taking care not to work too closely to skin. Chop pulp, and add one cup soft stale bread crumbs. Melt two tablespoons butter, add one half tablespoon finely chopped onion, and cook five minutes; or try out three slices of bacon, using bacon fat in place of butter. Add to chopped pulp and bread, season with salt and pepper, and if necessary moisten with a little stock or water; cook five minutes, cool slightly, and add one beaten egg. Refill egg plant, cover with buttered bread crumbs, and bake twenty-five minutes in a hot oven.

BAKED BANANAS.

Peel firm bananas and cut lengthwise; place in a baking dish. Slice a lemon very thin, put a layer of banana with three slices of lemon, and then a layer of banana and three slices of lemon, sprinkled well with sugar. Put in the oven to bake.

CROQUETTES OF FRENCH PEAS.

2 tablespoonfuls of butter.	2 tablespoonfuls of flour.
1 pint of cream.	Yelk of 1 egg.
2 cans of peas.	Salt, pepper, and celery salt.
1 teaspoonful onion juice.	

Melt butter and flour together, then add the cream and seasonings and the well-beaten yelk of egg, and then the peas, which have been put through a puree strainer. Pour out on to a platter to cool, roll into croquettes, and fry as chicken croquettes.

ENTREES.

CHICKEN WITH ASPARAGUS TIPS.

2 cups very tender chicken breast.	1 tablespoonful of butter.
1 cup cooked asparagus tips (fresh or canned).	1/2 pint cream.
	Yelks of 2 hard-boiled eggs,

Rub the yelks and butter to a paste and add the cream. Stir until thoroughly blended. Season with salt and pepper; then lay in the asparagus tips and chicken, and cook for a few minutes. Delicious patty filling.

SUPREME OF CHICKEN.

Breast and wing of one large chicken (raw), four eggs, two thirds of cup of thick cream; season with salt, pepper, and celery salt. Force chicken through meat grinder. Beat eggs separately and add, stirring until mixture is smooth. Add cream and seasoning. Butter timbal molds and line with chopped mushrooms, then fill with the chicken, and set molds in a pan of boiling water and bake about thirty minutes. Serve with bechamel sauce.

CHICKEN CROQUETTES.

Boil one chicken and grind the meat with one can mushrooms; soak one half pound stale bread in the broth and add to meat and mushrooms; add one quarter of a pound of butter and four eggs, mix all well together and boil until well cooked, season with salt, pepper, celery salt, chopped parsley, a little finely chopped onion, and a very little nutmeg. Pour out on a platter; when thoroughly cold, shape, roll in bread crumbs and fry in boiling fat.

STUFFED CHICKEN LEGS.

Breast of one chicken.	1 cup of cream.
Whites of 2 eggs.	3 tablespoons butter.
1 tablespoon onion.	3 tablespoons flour.

1 tablespoon fresh mushrooms.	1/2 teaspoon salt.
1 small truffle.	Little pepper.
	1 tablespoon sherry wine.

Melt butter, add chopped onion, mushrooms, and truffle, broil a few minutes. Remove onions, mushrooms, and truffle. Add flour, and when thoroughly blended add cream, salt, and pepper, cook until thick; then add the sherry wine. Add the onions, mushrooms, and truffle and the breast of a raw chicken, which has been ground and thoroughly mixed with the whites of two eggs; add to the other mixture. Spread out on a dish to cool. Remove bone from leg of the chicken (raw); fill with the mixture, sew up and broil in butter. Serve hot or cold. If served hot, serve with drawn butter. Delicious cold.

CHICKEN BREAST SMOTHERED IN MUSHROOMS.

Remove the breast from a chicken which has been partially boiled. Then remove the skin from the breast. Put in a pan with three tablespoons of butter, cover with fresh mushrooms and put in a hot oven. Cook until mushrooms are thoroughly done and breast is tender. Remove from the oven and add a little flour and cream to the butter in which chicken and mushrooms have been broiled; season with salt and pepper, and serve.

SWEETBREAD CROQUETTES.

2 pairs sweetbreads.	A few chopped mushrooms.
1 level tablespoonful of butter.	1 heaping tablespoon of flour,
1 cup of cream.	salt, pepper, and a little onion juice.

Parboil the sweetbreads, putting a little lemon juice in the water. Throw them into cold water. Remove the outside skin and membrane. Chop fine and measure. Add enough chopped mushrooms to make a pint. Melt the butter and add the flour and then the cream. When smooth, add the yelk of one egg. Season with salt, pepper, and a little onion juice, chopped parsley, and celery salt. Then add the sweetbreads and mushrooms. Cook a few minutes, turn out to cool, shape, dip in bread crumbs, diluted eggs and crumbs, place in a frying-basket and fry in hot lard.

SWEETBREAD A LA DIPLOMAT.

Saute one half tablespoon of chopped onion in two tablespoons of butter. Add two tablespoons of flour, one cup of white stock and cream, season with salt and cayenne. Add yelk of one egg. When it thickens, add one third cup of mushrooms, chopped fine, two tablespoons of chopped truffles, trimmings of the sweetbreads, and a little chopped parsley. Then add one tablespoon of sherry wine. Let it cool and spread on sweetbreads which have been sauted in butter (after parboiling), dip in eggs, bread crumbs and eggs, and fry in hot fat. Serve with allemande sauce.

SWEETBREAD CUTLETS.

Boil two pairs of sweetbreads in salt water with a tablespoonful of lemon juice; drain and cover with cold water. When cold, chop fine and add sufficient chopped mushrooms to make one pint in all. Melt one tablespoonful of butter, add one tablespoonful of flour, salt and pepper to taste. When smooth, add slowly a cup of cream. When this thickens, add a tablespoonful of lemon juice and a slight grating of nutmeg, half a teaspoon of finely chopped parsley, one beaten egg, and the sweetbreads and mushrooms. Pour out on a dish to cool, make palm shape, roll in bread crumbs, diluted egg and bread crumbs, place in frying basket and fry in hot lard. Serve with allemande sauce.

LITTLE PIGS IN BLANKETS.

Select large, plump oysters, or firm pieces of sweetbread which have been parboiled. Wrap them in thin slices of fat bacon, pinning with a wooden toothpick. Broil in a little butter.

STUFFED PEPPERS.

Cut off the tops of green peppers and remove the seed, parboil them ten minutes, chop the tops fine, one tablespoonful of chopped onion and two of fresh chopped mushrooms; saute all in two tablespoonfuls of butter about twelve minutes, add one tablespoon of flour, half a cup of brown stock, one tablespoon of ground chicken, one half tablespoon of ground ham, and one tablespoon of bread crumbs. Season with salt, pepper, and chopped parsley, cool, then stuff the peppers, sprinkle with buttered bread crumbs and put in the oven to brown; serve with white sauce.

STUFFED MUSHROOMS.

Cut off the caps, peel, scrape out, and saute in butter. Then chop fine a little onion, and two tablespoons of chopped mushrooms, and saute in two tablespoons of butter. Add one heaping tablespoon of flour, one third of a cup of brown stock, and one quarter of a cup of cream. Season with salt, cayenne, and chopped parsley, and when thick, add a little ground chicken, ground ham, and sweetbreads. When cold, put through pastry bag on to mushrooms, cover with buttered bread crumbs, and put in oven to brown. Serve on round toast with mushroom sauce.

PEPPER TIMBALS.

Butter well a tin timbal mold or cup, line with a large red pepper from which has been taken the seeds (and which has been parboiled, or use the canned red pepper), butter them and line with chopped mushrooms. Drop into each one a raw egg, sprinkle over a little salt and pepper, put into a baking pan which is half full of boiling water, and put into a hot oven and cook until the egg is thoroughly done. Turn out and serve with white sauce.

MUSHROOMS A L'ALGONQUIN.

Wash, peel, and remove the stems from large, selected mushrooms and then saute in butter; when done, put in a buttered pan, placing on each a large oyster; sprinkle with salt and pepper, place on each a bit of butter, cook in a hot oven until the oysters are plump. Serve with drawn butter sauce.

EGGS A LA TURK.

Brown one chicken liver and one large mushroom together in butter one minute. Add a little chopped onion salt and pepper, and a tablespoonful of flour; beat until smooth. Then add one tablespoon of sherry and enough brown stock to make a sauce—about half a cupful—one teaspoonful of lemon juice, and a few chopped truffles. Place a poached egg, well cooked, on round buttered toast, and serve the sauce around it.

SAUCES.

ALLEMANDE SAUCE.

Melt two level tablespoonfuls of butter, and add two heaping tablespoonfuls of flour; when smooth, pour on one half pint of white stock and one half pint of cream; season with salt, pepper, chopped parsley, and lemon juice, and then add the beaten yelk of an egg.

BECHAMEL SAUCE.

1 1/2 cups white stock.	1 slice of onion.
1 slice of carrot.	1 bay leaf.
1 sprig of parsley.	1/4 cup of butter.
1/4 cup of flour.	1 cup of cream.
Salt and pepper.	

Cook the stock with the onion, carrot, bay leaf, and parsley about fifteen minutes, and then strain. Melt the butter, add the flour, then the stock and cream.

WHITE SAUCE.

2 tablespoons butter;	1 cup milk.
2 tablespoons flour.	1/4 teaspoon salt.
Few grains pepper.	

Put butter in saucepan, stir until melted and bubbling; add flour mixed with seasonings, and stir until thoroughly blended. Pour on gradually the milk, adding about one third at a time, stirring until well mixed, then beating until smooth and glossy. If a wire whisk is used, all the milk may be added at once; and although more quickly made if milk is scalded, it is not necessary.

HOLLANDAISE SAUCE.

1/2 cup of butter.	1/2 teaspoon of salt.
Yelks of 4 uncooked eggs.	1/3 cup of boiling water.
1 1/2 tablespoonfuls lemon juice.	Dash of cayenne.

Fill a bowl with hot water, pour out the water and wipe the bowl dry. Put the butter into it and beat until soft and creamy; add the yelks of the eggs, one by one, and beat until they are blended with the butter. Add the lemon juice, salt, and pepper, and beat again until smooth. Then take out the spoon and beat the mixture with an egg beater five minutes. Put into a double boiler with boiling water. Add to the butter and eggs one third cup of boiling water and cook until the same is as thick as mayonnaise, beating constantly with the egg beater. Serve either hot or cold.

MUSHROOM SAUCE.

Two tablespoons of butter, two and one half tablespoons of flour, one cup of brown stock, one half slice of onion, one quarter can of mushrooms, cut up. Cook onion in butter until slightly browned, and remove onion. Add flour and seasonings, and then add stock gradually, and when perfectly smooth add mushrooms.

HORSERADISH SAUCE.

Mix two tablespoonfuls of grated horseradish with one tablespoonful of vinegar and one fourth teaspoonful each of salt and pepper. Mix thoroughly and stir in four tablespoonfuls of whipped cream, stiff. Serve with roast beef or oysters.

CUCUMBER SAUCE.

1 large cucumber.	1/2 cup whipped cream.
4 drops of onion juice.	1/2 teaspoon salt.
1/2 teaspoon of parsley.	Few grains pepper.
1/2 teaspoon Tarragon vinegar.	

Chop fine one large cucumber, add salt and cayenne pepper to taste, add onion juice, parsley chopped fine, vinegar, and whipped cream.

LOBSTER SAUCE.

2 tablespoonfuls of butter.	2 tablespoonfuls of flour.
1 pint of cream.	Yelks of 2 eggs.

Season with salt, pepper, and a little sherry wine. Melt the butter, then add the flour, then the cream, then the seasoning, and then the well-beaten yelks, and when thick add a heaping cup of lobster, chopped fine.

MINT SAUCE.

1/4 cup finely chopped mint leaves.   1 tablespoon powdered sugar.
1/2 cup vinegar.

Add sugar to vinegar; when dissolved, pour over mint and let stand thirty minutes on back of range to infuse. If vinegar is very strong dilute with water.

MAÎTRE D'HÔTEL BUTTER.

1/4 cup butter.	1/8 teaspoon pepper.
1/2 teaspoon salt.	1/2 tablespoon finely chopped
3/4 tablespoon lemon juice.	parsley.

Put butter in a bowl, and with small wooden spoon work until creamy. Add salt, pepper, and parsley, then lemon juice very slowly.

TOMATO SAUCE I (Without Stock).

1/2 can tomatoes, or	3 tablespoons butter.
1 3/4 cups fresh stewed tomatoes.	2 1/2 tablespoons flour.
1 slice onion.	1/4 teaspoon salt.
1/8 teaspoon pepper.	

Cook onion with tomatoes fifteen minutes, rub through a strainer, and add to butter and flour (to which seasonings have been added) cooked together. If tomatoes are very acid add a few grains of soda.

TOMATO SAUCE II.

1/2 can tomatoes.	1/2 teaspoon salt.
2 teaspoons sugar.	4 tablespoons butter.
8 peppercorns.	4 tablespoons flour.
Bit of bay leaf.	1 cup brown stock.

Cook tomatoes twenty minutes with sugar, peppercorns, bay leaf, and salt; rub through a strainer and add stock. Brown the butter, add flour, and when well browned gradually add hot liquid.

SALADS.

CUCUMBER, CELERY, AND SWEETBREAD SALAD.

Equal proportions of cucumber, celery, and sweetbreads, which have been parboiled. Cut into small pieces and serve with mayonnaise or French dressing. Garnish with water cress or serve in head lettuce.

CUCUMBER AND CELERY SALAD.

Equal proportions of cucumber and celery. Cut cucumber and celery into small pieces and serve with mayonnaise dressing.

FROZEN TOMATO SALAD.

Take one quart can of tomatoes (or the same proportion of fresh tomatoes), drain off all the liquor, pour over them mayonnaise and a little chopped celery, put in a freezer and freeze. Serve in nasturtium leaves.

CHICKEN SALAD.

Take equal proportions of cold chicken and celery, cut not too small. To a quart of chicken and celery pour over one half cup of French dressing and let it marinate half or whole morning, and when ready to serve mix with mayonnaise dressing.

NUT AND CELERY SALAD.

Mix equal parts of pecans, almonds, English walnuts, and celery. Marinate in oil, and serve with a French dressing with a border of curly celery.

TOMATOES STUFFED WITH CHEESE.

Take equal proportions of Neufchatel and Roquefort cheese and blend well together; mix with mayonnaise dressing. Remove centers out of tomatoes, fill with the cheese and serve on lettuce leaf.

PINEAPPLE AND NUT SALAD.

1 can pineapple.   1 cup English walnuts.

Remove the juice from the pineapple, cut into pieces about the size of an English walnut; add the walnuts and serve with whipped cream or mayonnaise.

WALDORF SALAD.

Mix equal quantities of finely cut apple and celery, and moisten with mayonnaise dressing. Garnish with curled celery and canned pimentoes cut in strips or fancy shapes. An attractive way of serving this salad is to remove tops from red or green apples, scoop out inside pulp, leaving just enough adhering to skin to keep apples in shape. Refill shells thus made with the salad, replace tops, and serve on lettuce leaves.

LOBSTER SALAD.

1 cup of boiled lobster.   1/2 cup chopped celery.

Mix together and serve with mayonnaise dressing. Serve in lobster shell, red apples, or lettuce leaf.

WATER CRESS SALAD.

Freshen the water cress in very cold water until it becomes crisp. Dry thoroughly without bruising. Mix with it two sour apples sliced thin and French dressing.

PEPPER AND GRAPE FRUIT SALAD.

Cut slices from stem ends of six green peppers, and remove seeds. Refill with grape fruit pulp, finely cut celery, and English walnut meats broken in pieces, allowing twice as much grape fruit as celery, and two nut meats to each pepper. Arrange on chicory or lettuce leaves and serve.

SWISS SALAD.

Mix one cup cold cooked chicken, cut in cubes, one cucumber pared and cut in cubes, one cup chopped English walnut meats, and one cup French peas. Marinate with French dressing, arrange on serving dish, and garnish with mayonnaise dressing.

GREEN GRAPE SALAD.

Select firm, acid grapes; serve in a head of lettuce with the cooked mayonnaise, only with a little more cream added to it, or with a cream dressing, for which mix half a teaspoonful of salt, half a teaspoonful of mustard, one fourth teaspoonful of sugar, one egg beaten slightly, two tablespoonfuls of oil, three fourths cup of rich cream, and a scant quarter of a cup of vinegar.

TOMATO JELLY.

Cook one half can of tomatoes for ten minutes, with a pinch of soda if very acid. Add half a teaspoonful of salt and rub through a sieve or strainer. Pour over it one fourth box of gelatine which has been soaked in one fourth cup of cold water; mold, and when congealed, serve on lettuce with mayonnaise dressing.

SALAD A LA JARDINE.

To one pint of ground, boiled chicken, add equal parts of asparagus tips, peas, chopped string beans, chopped celery, and a few pecan kernels. Mix carefully and pour over it mayonnaise.

EGG SALAD.

Boil the eggs twenty minutes. Peel off the shells and cut the eggs in half lengthwise. Remove the yelks, put in a bowl and cream. Take two eggs well beaten, half a teaspoonful of dry mustard, three tablespoonfuls of rich, sweet cream, one tablespoonful of salt, one teaspoonful of pepper, two tablespoonfuls of olive oil, and one and a half tablespoonfuls of vinegar. Boil all until very thick and mix with the cooked yelks. Fill the whites, and when cold serve with mayonnaise.

SALAD DRESSINGS.

MAYONNAISE No. 1.

Yelk of 1 hard-boiled egg.	1 teaspoonful of mustard.
Salt and pepper to taste.	Yelk of 1 raw egg, well beaten.
1/2 of small bottle olive oil.	Vinegar to taste.
White of 1 egg beaten stiff and dry.	

Rub the yelk of hard-boiled egg through a fine sieve until smooth; add to that the mustard, salt, pepper, raw yelk, well beaten. Then add the oil, and next the vinegar slowly, lastly the raw white of egg.

MAYONNAISE No. 2 (COOKED).

Yelks of two eggs, well beaten, four tablespoonfuls of vinegar. Boil until thick, and stir in one heaping tablespoonful of butter or olive oil. When cold, add half a teaspoonful of salt, half a teaspoonful of dry mustard and a little pepper, and a cup of whipped cream.

POTATO MAYONNAISE DRESSING.

1 small baked potato.	1 teaspoon powdered sugar.
1 teaspoon mustard.	2 tablespoons vinegar.
1 teaspoon salt.	3/4 cup olive oil or Snowflake oil.

Smooth and mash the inside of a potato, add mustard, salt, and powdered sugar; add one tablespoon of vinegar, and rub mixture through a fine sieve. Add oil and remaining vinegar. One would hardly realize eggs were not used in the mixture.

DRESSING FOR COLE SLAW.

6 yelks of eggs.	2 tablespoons of fine sugar.
Tablespoon butter.	1 cup of vinegar.
Teaspoon of made mustard.	1/2 teaspoon of salt.

Beat the eggs well. Cook in a double boiler with vinegar, sugar, butter, salt, and mustard, beating all the time. When nearly done, add the juice of one lemon. When thick remove from the fire and when cold whip in one half cupful of cream. Mix well, and put in a cold place until ready to serve.

GERMAN DRESSING.

Beat one half cup of heavy cream, just beginning to sour, with one egg; beat until stiff. Add three tablespoonfuls of vinegar and beat again. Fine for fruit salads.

FRENCH DRESSING.

1/2 teaspoon salt.	2 tablespoons of vinegar.
1/4 teaspoon pepper.	4 tablespoons of oil.

Mix ingredients and stir until well blended.

NOTE.—2 drops of creme de menthe added to French dressing makes a delicious dressing; and very crisp bacon added to French dressing makes a delicious dressing for lettuce.

SALAD CREAM.

Mix one half tablespoonful of mustard and salt (each) and one tablespoonful of sugar with one egg, slightly beaten. Pour on this three fourths cup of cream and one fourth cup of scalded vinegar with two and a half tablespoonfuls melted butter. Cook in a double boiler until it thickens slightly. Strain and cool. Serve on cold slaw.

SANDWICHES.

In preparing sandwiches cut the slices of bread as thin as possible and remove the crusts. If butter is used, cream the butter and spread the bread before cutting from the loaf.

LETTUCE SANDWICH.

Spread bread with mayonnaise dressing and then place sliced lettuce between the slices.

CHICKEN SALAD SANDWICH.

Cut up equal proportions of chicken and celery fine. Mix with mayonnaise dressing and spread between plain bread.

PLAIN GROUND CHICKEN.

Grind chicken fine, moisten thoroughly with cream, season with salt, pepper, and celery salt and spread between buttered bread.

NUT SANDWICHES.

Spread bread with mayonnaise dressing, and put chopped pecans between the slices.

CUCUMBER SANDWICHES.

Chop the cucumber, mix with tartar sauce and spread between bread.

RUSSIAN SANDWICH.

Spread Graham bread with mayonnaise dressing. Take equal parts of Neufchatel cheese and chopped olives and mix well together and spread between slices of bread.

PEANUT SANDWICH.

Spread bread (white or Graham bread) with French mustard. Pound roasted peanuts to a paste and spread between the slices.

CHEESE AND NUT.

Spread bread with mayonnaise dressing; mix Neufchatel cheese and nuts well together and spread between bread.

FIG SANDWICH.

Chop one dozen figs very fine, add hot water to moisten to a paste, cook in a double boiler two hours, flavor to taste with lemon. Put between thin slices of bread. Sprinkle with chopped nuts.

CLUB SANDWICH.

Spread toasted white bread with mayonnaise dressing, then a lettuce leaf, a slice of crisp bacon, and a small slice of cold chicken between the slices of toast.

DESSERTS.

PLAIN PASTRY.

1 1/2 cups flour.
1/4 cup lard.
A little ice water.

1/4 cup of butter.
1/2 teaspoonful salt.

Wash the butter, squeeze out all the milk and water, flatten it out. Add the salt to the flour and cut in the lard with a knife. Moisten it with the cold water. Toss on the board, dredged sparingly with flour, pat and roll out. Fold in the butter, roll out, and repeat folding and rolling several times. Cover with cheesecloth and set away in a cool place, though never in direct contact with ice. Roll thin and bake in a moderate oven.

FILLING FOR LEMON PIE.

2 lemons.
2 cups of sugar.
2 cups of hot water.

3 tablespoons flour.
1 tablespoon butter.
4 eggs.

Whites for top of pies. Boil until thick, bake crust and fill. Filling makes two pies.

COCOANUT FILLING.

One half of a cup of butter, two cups of sugar, mixed well. Add the yelks of five eggs well beaten, one cup of milk, one tablespoon of flour, and one cup of grated cocoa- nut. Flavor with vanilla and cook until thick. When cold, fill (cooked) pie crust and cover with meringue and put in the oven to brown.

BUTTERMILK PIES.

1 pint of buttermilk.
2 teacups of sugar.
1 tablespoon butter.

1 teaspoon cream of tartar.
3 tablespoons of flour.
5 to 7 eggs.

Use whites for the meringue. Boil this to a custard and fill the pie crusts and bake.

MERINGUE.

Add sugar enough to the whites to make thick and stiff; spread over pies and put in oven to brown a few minutes.

SUGAR PIES.

Four eggs beaten separately, one pint of brown sugar, one tablespoon of butter, one cup of cream. Boil all together and when thick fill the pastry and bake.

JELLY PIES.

4 eggs beaten separately.	1 glass of jelly (plum jelly best).
1 1/2 cups of sugar.	1 tablespoon of flour.
1 tablespoon of butter.	

Mix the butter and sugar together, then flour, then the jelly, then the eggs. Beat well and fill pastry and bake.

ENGLISH PLUM PUDDING.

1/2 pound stale bread crumbs.	1/2 cup wine and brandy mixed.
1/4 pound sugar.	1 cup hot milk.
1/2 nutmeg, grated.	1 teaspoonful cinnamon.
1/2 teaspoonful mace and ground cloves.	4 eggs.
	1/2 pound beef suet.
1 teaspoonful salt.	1/4 pound currants.
1 1/2 pounds raisins.	1/8 pound citron.
1/4 pound figs.	

Soak the stale bread crumbs in one cup of hot milk. When cold, add the sugar and yelks of eggs beaten stiff, also nutmeg, cinnamon, mace, ground cloves, and salt. Chop fine and cream the beef suet and add to the mixture with the raisins stoned and floured, and the currants, figs, and citron chopped fine. Add the wine and brandy, and the whites of four eggs beaten stiff. Turn into a buttered mold and steam from six to eight hours. — *Boston Cooking School.*

MINCEMEAT PATTIES.

Heat patty shells and mincemeat separately. When very hot, fill the shells with the mincemeat and serve with frozen whipped cream, flavored with brandy.

FIG PUDDING.

1/3 pound beef suet.	1 teaspoonful salt.
2 heaping cups stale bread crumbs.	1/2 pound figs.
1/2 cup milk.	2 eggs well beaten.
1 cup sugar.	

Chop and rub to a cream the beef suet, add the raisins finely chopped; mix thoroughly. To the bread crumbs add the well-beaten eggs, milk, sugar, and salt, and mix all together well. Place in a buttered pudding dish and steam for several hours. Serve with a fancy sauce.

SAUCE FOR SAME.

Beat the yelks of two eggs until light. Then beat the whites of two eggs stiff and add half a cup of powdered sugar. Combine the two and add one fourth cup of hot cream and four tablespoonfuls sherry wine. — *Boston Cooking School.*

CABINET PUDDING.

1 pint of milk.	1/2 cup raisins, chopped citron,
2 tablespoonfuls of sugar.	currants.
1/2 tablespoonful of butter.	1/4 teaspoonful of salt.
2 eggs.	1 1/2 pints stale sponge cake.

Beat the eggs, sugar, and salt together; add the milk; sprinkle a pudding mold with cake crumbs, then a layer of fruit, then cake crumbs, and continue until all is used up. Pour on the custard and let it stand two hours, then steam one and a half hours.

SAUCE FOR SAME.

1 cup of butter.	1/2 cup of cream.	2 cups powdered sugar.

Beat the butter to a cream, add the sugar gradually, and when very light, add the cream.. Flavor to taste. Cook for a few minutes in a double boiler.

RICE PUDDING.

4 tablespoonfuls of rice.	Milk and cream.
1/2 teaspoonful of salt.	4 tablespoonfuls sugar.
1 teaspoonful vanilla.	1/2 cup of stoned raisins.

Into a pudding-dish holding a quart put the rice, which has been well washed and soaked. Fill the dish with milk and cream, and add the salt. Put into the oven to cook for about half an hour. Add the sugar, vanilla, and raisins, and return to the oven and cook slowly for two hours or more if necessary. If the milk boils down, lift the skin at the side and add a little more hot cream. To make the pudding creamy it must be cooked very slowly and plenty of cream used. Just before serving, spread thickly over the top fresh marshmallows. Put in the oven just long enough for the marshmallows to swell. Before sending to the table, garnish with candied cherries or red jelly. Served with whipped or plain cream.

PINEAPPLE PUDDING.

2 3/4 cups of scalded cream.	1/4 cup of sugar.
1/3 cup of corn starch.	1/2 can grated pineapple.
1/4 teaspoonful of salt.	Whites of three eggs, beaten
1/4 cup of cold milk.	stiff.

Mix the corn starch, sugar, salt, and cold milk well, and add to the scalded cream in a double boiler, stirring constantly until it thickens. Cook from ten to fifteen minutes, add the eggs, then pineapple. Mold, congeal, and serve with whipped cream.

BAVARIAN CREAM.

1/3 box of gelatine.	1/2 cup of boiling water.
Sweeten and flavor to taste.	1 quart of whipped cream.

Soak the gelatine in the boiling water, sweeten and flavor to taste; add one quart of stiff whipped cream; put in molds and set away to congeal, and serve with whipped cream.

CHARLOTTE RUSSE.

White of 1 egg.	Sponge lady fingers.
1/3 box gelatine dissolved in 1/2 pint boiling water.	1 cup powdered sugar.
	2 teaspoonfuls vanilla.
Yelks of 3 eggs.	Whip from 1 quart of cream.

Beat the white of an egg slightly, put a thin coating around a glass bowl, and then line with sponge lady fingers. Dissolve the gelatine in boiling water. When thoroughly dissolved, stir in the sugar, add the vanilla and the beaten yelks of three eggs ; stir in the whip from a quart of cream, and when it stiffens some, pour into the bowl lined with sponge cakes and garnish the top prettily with whipped cream.

BAKED CARAMEL CUSTARD WITH SAUCE.

Set a small saucepan, containing one half cup of sugar, over the fire and stir the sugar gently. As the sugar loses water by evaporation it assumes the appearance of flake tapioca, and as the cooking continues it changes color, becoming caramel. Care must be taken that the caramel does not burn or become too dark in color. Scald four cups of milk, and add the caramel to the milk very carefully, and as soon as the two are well blended, pour the mixture on to five eggs slightly beaten; then add one half teaspoonful of salt and one teaspoonful of vanilla. Strain at once into a buttered melon mold, set the mold in a pan of hot water and bake in a slow oven until the custard is firm. Serve with caramel sauce.

SAUCE FOR SAME.

Put one half cup of sugar into a saucepan over the fire and stir the sugar until it melts and becomes a light brown color. Add half a cup of boiling water, and allow the liquid to simmer ten minutes.

STRAWBERRY SPONGE.

Soak one third box of gelatine in one third cup of cold water; dissolve in one third cup of boiling water; add one cup of sugar, juice

74

of one lemon, and one cup of strawberry juice. Set vessel in a pan of ice water and stir until it thickens. Add the whites of three eggs beaten stiff ; and whip from one pint of cream. Chill before serving. The cream may be omitted. If preserved strawberries are used less sugar is required.

COMPOTE OF FIGS.

One pint of figs scalded and soaked over night in brandy. Pile up on a platter and serve with whipped cream or serve with brandy.

BANBURY TARTS.

1 cup raisins.	1 egg.
1 cup sugar.	1 cracker.
Juice and grated rind 1 lemon.	

Stone and chop raisins, add sugar, egg slightly beaten, cracker finely rolled, and lemon juice and rind. Roll pastry one-eighth inch thick, and cut pieces three and one half inches long by three inches wide. Put two teaspoons of mixture on each piece. Moisten edge with cold water half way round, fold over, press edges together with three-tined fork, first dipped in flour. Bake twenty minutes in slow oven.

SIMPLE DESSERT.

Lady fingers.	Bananas, sliced thin.
1/2 cup of sherry wine.	2 heaping tablespoonfuls of sugar.
Whipped cream.	

Line a bowl with lady fingers, fill it half full of bananas sliced thin, pour over them about half a cup of sherry wine and a heaping tablespoonful of sugar, then fill the bowl with whipped cream.

PRESERVES IN HALF ORANGES.

Take half of an orange, scoop out all of the pulp, cut the edge in points, fill in with preserves—pineapple being prettiest—and serve with whipped cream.

CAKES.

* FRUIT CAKE.

1 pound butter.	2 pounds raisins.
1 pound sugar.	1 pound currants.
1 pound flour.	1/2 pound figs.
1/2 pound citron.	1/2 pound pineapple.
1/2 pound candied cherries.	2 pounds almonds.
12 eggs.	1 tablespoon cinnamon.
2 nutmegs.	1 tablespoon allspice.
1/2 glass of wine.	1 cup of molasses.
1/2 glass of brandy.	2 teaspoons baking powder.

Cream the butter and sugar together. Add New Orleans molasses, then eggs, which have been beaten separately, next the flour, which has been browned; then dissolve two teaspoons of baking powder in a cup of cream or new milk, and add to the mixture. Then add the spices which have been dissolved in the tumblerful of liquor. Chop fruit and nuts, dredge with flour, and put in the batter last. Bake slowly four hours.

PECAN CAKE.

1 pound sugar.	1 pound flour.
1 pound of butter.	10 eggs.
1/2 tumbler of brandy.	2 grated nutmegs.
1 pound of raisins.	1/4 pound of citron.

1 1/2 pound of pecan kernels.

Cream the butter and sugar until light. Add the eggs beaten separately, then the nutmeg stirred in the brandy, then the flour, raisins, citron, and pecan kernels. Pour into buttered mold and bake half an hour longer than you would a black cake, same size.

IMPERIAL CAKE.

1 pound butter.	1 pound light brown sugar.

* NOTE. — This is the recipe which gave me my start in business.

1 pound flour.   2 pounds raisins.
10 eggs.   2 pounds blanched almonds.
6 grated nutmegs.   1/2 pound citron.

Cream the butter and flour together, beat the yelks and sugar together, add the whites well beaten, mix them with the flour and butter. After this is all well beaten dredge fruit well with flour and put it in by degrees, add wine glass of whisky or brandy. Bake in a loaf for four hours.

WHITE LADY CAKE.

12 eggs.   2 1/2 teacups sugar.
1 teacup of butter.   3 1/2 teacups of flour.
1/2 cup of cream.   3 teaspoonfuls baking powder.

Cream the butter and sugar together until very light; add the whites of eggs beaten stiff, then the flour, and then the baking powder stirred in the cream. Bake in a solid cake in a moderate oven for very nearly one hour. Any desired flavoring may be used.

LAYER CAKE.

1 cup butter.   6 eggs.
3 cups flour.   2 heaping teaspoons baking
1/2 cup milk.   powder.
              2 cups sugar.

Take only the whites of eggs, beaten stiff. Mix as in lady cake, and bake in tins in a moderate oven.

SPONGE CAKE.

12 eggs.   1 1/3 cups of sugar.
1 1/3 cups flour.   1 level teaspoonful cream tartar.

Beat the yelks of eight eggs with the sugar until very light. Beat the whites of twelve eggs with the cream tartar to a stiff froth. Add to the yelks and sugar, then add the flour slowly; flavor to taste, and bake in a moderate oven forty minutes.

ANGEL FOOD.

12 eggs, whites beaten stiff.	1 teaspoonful cream tartar.
1 1/2 tumblers powdered sugar.	1 tumbler of flour.

Take the whites of eggs beaten to a stiff froth with the cream of tartar added. Sift the powdered sugar into the eggs and cut it in with an egg-beater (never stir angel food with a spoon). After the flour has been sifted five times, sift very slowly into the egg and sugar. Add a teaspoonful of vanilla. Grease the cake pan very little with butter, lining the bottom with unglazed letter paper which has been slightly greased. Pour in the cake and bake forty minutes. Put a pan of water over it from the first. Remove from the oven, invert the pan, and let it stand until the cake falls out without being disturbed.

HICKORY NUT CAKE.

1/2 cup butter.	1 cup granulated sugar.
3 eggs.	1 cup milk.
1 1/2 cups flour.	1 1/2 teaspoons baking powder.
1 cup hickory nuts chopped fine.	

Cream the butter and add the sugar gradually. Beat the yelks of three eggs light and add to the butter and sugar with one cup milk. To the flour add the baking powder, stir into the batter, add the hickory nut meats chopped fine, and the whites of two eggs beaten stiff. Bake in a buttered and floured pan from forty to fifty minutes, or in small pans.

DEVILS' FOOD.

Whites 8 eggs.	1 cup of butter.
3 cups sugar.	1 cup sweet or sour milk.
3 cups flour.	1/2 cup grated chocolate melted.

Cream the butter and sugar together; add the chocolate, then the eggs. If sweet milk is used, use two teaspoons of baking powder. If buttermilk is used, use one teaspoon of soda. Whichever is used, add next to the mixture and lastly the flour. Bake in solid mold.

ICING.

Two cups of granulated sugar, one cup of brown sugar, three fourths cup of grated chocolate, one cup rich cream, tablespoon of butter cooked until done; add vanilla and beat until it begins to thicken.

SPICE CAKE.

1 cup of sugar.	1/2 cup of molasses.
1/2 cup of butter.	1/2 cup of sour milk.
2 1/2 cups of flour.	1 teaspoonful of soda.
1 tablespoonful cinnamon.	1 tablespoonful ginger.
4 eggs.	1/2 teaspoonful of cloves.
1/2 teaspoonful allspice.	1 1/2 pounds raisins (if desired).

Use only the well-beaten yelks of eggs. Bake in small pans or as a solid cake.

MUFFIN CAKES.

1 cup of butter.	3 cups of flour.
2 cups of sugar.	4 eggs.

Cream the butter and sugar together, beat eggs separately, add the yelks and then the whites. Dissolve two teaspoons of baking powder in one half cup of milk, add to the batter, and lastly the flour. Bake in muffin rings.

BLACKBERRY JAM CAKE.

3/4 cup of butter.	3 eggs.
1 cup of sugar.	1 cup of jam.
2 cups of flour.	3 tablespoons of cream.
2 teaspoons of cinnamon.	1 teaspoon baking powder.
1 teaspoon nutmeg.	1 teaspoon cloves.
1 teaspoon allspice.	

Cream the butter and sugar, add the jam, then the eggs beaten separately, add the spices and then the baking powder dissolved in the cream, and lastly the flour. Bake in layers. Put white icing between and all over it.

SOUR MILK GINGER BREAD.

1 cup molasses.
2 1/3 cups flour.
2 teaspoonfuls ginger.

1 cup sour milk.
1 3/4 teaspoonfuls soda.
1/2 teaspoonful salt.

1/4 cup melted butter.

Add the milk to the molasses, mix and sift the dry ingredients, combine the two, add butter and beat vigorously. Pour into a buttered, shallow pan and bake twenty- five minutes in a moderate oven.

GINGER SNAPS.

2 cups of molasses.
1 cup of lard.

1 heaping teaspoon ginger.
1/2 teaspoon pepper.

1 tablespoon of soda.

Cream the molasses and lard together; add ginger and pepper, then dissolve the soda in as little hot water as possible and add flour enough to roll. Roll thin, cut out and bake in buttered pans with a little flour sprinkled over them.

GINGER BREAD.

1 cup molasses.
1 3/4 teaspoonfuls soda.
1 egg.
2 teaspoonfuls ginger.

1/3 cup of butter.
1/2 cup sour milk.
2 cups flour.
1/2 teaspoonful of salt.

Put the butter and molasses in a saucepan and cook until the boiling point is reached. Remove from the fire, add the soda and beat vigorously, then add the milk, eggs well beaten, and the remaining ingredients mixed and sifted. Bake fifteen minutes in buttered pans two thirds filled with the mixture.

COOKIES.

3 cups sugar.
6 eggs.

1 1/2 cups butter.
5 pints flour.

3 teaspoonfuls carbonate of ammonia.

Cream the butter and sugar, beat the eggs three at a time into it, and then beat well. Add the ammonia, and lastly flour, and roll thin.

SAND TARTS.

1 cup butter.	2 cups sugar.
3 eggs.	Flour enough to roll.

Roll thin, paint the tops with the white of egg, sprinkle over with equal parts of ground cinnamon and granulated sugar, and in the center of each place one fourth of a blanched almond. Put in floured pans and bake in a quick oven.

CRULLERS.

2 cups of butter.	3 1/2 cups of sugar.
12 eggs.	Flour enough to roll.

Flavor with nutmeg or cinnamon, roll thin, shape and fry in hot fat.

NURRUMBURGHS.

2 eggs.	1/3 teaspoon ground cinnamon.
1/2 cup sugar.	1/8 teaspoon ground cloves.
3/4 cup flour.	2/3 cup roasted almonds.
1/4 teaspoon salt.	1 tablespoon candied orange peel.
	Grated rind of 1/2 of lemon.

Beat whites of two eggs stiff, add one cup of sugar and yelks of two eggs, three fourths cup of flour, one fourth teaspoon salt, one third teaspoon cinnamon, one eighth teaspoon cloves, two thirds cup roasted almonds. Drop on sheet sprinkled with one half sugar and one half com starch. Sprinkle top with chopped almonds, cut out and bake.

FILLINGS FOR CAKES.

PLAIN CARAMEL.

2 cups of sugar.	3/4 cup of maple syrup.
Cream to wet thoroughly.	1 tablespoonful butter.

81

Put sugar, syrup, and cream on, and when it boils add the butter. Boil it until very thick. Add one teaspoonful of vanilla, take from the fire, and beat until it begins to sugar. Then pour over the cake.

CHOCOLATE CARAMEL.

Same as above, only before it begins to boil add one fourth cake of Baker's chocolate.

SOUR CREAM FILLING.

Blanch one half pound almonds and chop them. Beat a teacup of sour cream until light and thick; add three tablespoonfuls of sugar, two eggs beaten separately, and the chopped nuts. Hickory or any kind of nuts can be used. Spread between layers of cake.

ICE CREAM FILLING.

3 cups sugar.	1 cup water.
3 eggs, whites beaten stiff.	1 teaspoonful vanila.

Boil sugar and water to a candy, pour slowly over the beaten whites of three eggs, flavor with vanilla, beat until it begins to cream, and pour over the cake.

Grated cocoanut sprinkled between the layers and on top makes a delicious cocoanut cake.

Blanched almonds grated and mixed with the icing makes a delicious filling.

MARSHMALLOW AND PINEAPPLE FILLING.

Take fresh marshmallows, put into the oven to soften, spread over the cake with a little chopped candied pineapple, and pour over same the ice cream filling given above.

CREAM ICING FOR ANGEL FOOD.

3 cups of sugar.	1/2 teaspoonful of vanilla.	1 cup of cream.

Let it come to a good hard boil, beat hard until creamy, and pour over the angel food.

PRAULINE ICING.

Make a plain caramel, and when done add one cup of broken pecan kernels just before pouring on the cake.

ICES.

NESSELBRODE PUDDING.

1 cup of marons.	1 cup of granulated sugar.
Yelks of 3 eggs.	1/2 pint of cream.
1/4 pound of candied fruits.	1/2 can pineapple (drained).

Take candied fruits and marons and soak them in sherry wine. Put sugar on the fire with one fourth of a cup of boiling water and boil to a syrup. Beat the yelks of eggs until light. Pour on them slowly the syrup, stirring all the time. Put on the fire in a double boiler and cook until the consistency of thick cream. Remove and beat hard until cold. When cold, add the cream, the marons pounded, and half a teaspoonful of vanilla, and freeze. When nearly hard frozen, add the candied fruits, one fourth of a pound of raisins, one fourth of a pound of pounded almonds, and a glass of sherry wine, and freeze hard. Remove the dasher and allow it to stand for several hours. — *Century Cook Book.*

PLAIN VANILLA CREAM.

Take one quart of plain, rich cream, season and flavor. When half frozen, add one quart of stiff whipped cream which has been sweetened and flavored. Freeze hard. Pack for an hour before using.

SULTANA ROLL.

Line a mold with pistachio ice cream, sprinkle with Sultana raisins, fill center with whipped cream, and let stand two and one half hours. Pack in ice and salt. Serve with claret sauce.

PISTACHIO ICE CREAM.

Scald one pint of cream. Mix one tablespoon of flour, one cup of sugar, one fourth teaspoon salt, and one beaten egg; pour on one pint of milk; cook twenty minutes in double boiler, stirring often. Cool.

Add one quart of cream flavored with one tablespoon of vanilla, tablespoon of almonds. Strain and freeze. Use just enough of Burnett's Fruit Coloring to make a pretty green.

CLARET SAUCE.

Boil one cup sugar and one third cup water to a syrup. Cool and add five tablespoonfuls claret.

TO FREEZE A WATERMELON.

Take three pints of stiff whipped cream, color with Burnett's Green Vegetable Coloring, sweeten and flavor with extract of pistachio, put in a freezer and freeze very hard.

Then take a quart of very stiff whipped cream, sweeten and flavor with a little sherry wine, put in a freezer and freeze hard.

Then take a quart of stiff whipped cream, sweeten and color pink with Burnett's Vegetable Coloring, and flavor with strawberry. Put in a freezer and freeze hard.

Take a melon mold and line it with the green, then put a layer of the white, and then the pink, sprinkled well with Sultana raisins that have been soaked in brandy, making the seeds. Cover with the white cream, and then the green; put a piece of buttered letter paper over it and then the tin top. Pack in salt and ice, and let stand for several hours.

FROZEN APRICOTS.

Cut one can of apricots in small pieces, drain and add to the syrup water enough to make a quart, add one and one half cups of sugar and cook ten minutes. Cool— partially freeze—add apricots and finish freezing. Pack the freezer with crushed ice and rock salt in proportions of three to one.

THREE OF A KIND.

Juice of 3 lemons.	Juice of 3 oranges.
Sugar to taste.	3 slices of canned peaches or
2 bananas.	pineapple.
1 quart of cold water.	

Take the lemon juice, cold water, and sugar, and a pint of rich cream—to be added after the lemon and water are packed in the freezer. When this begins to freeze, add the juice of three oranges, two bananas which have been put through a fine sieve, and three slices of canned peaches or pineapple put through a sieve. Freeze until very hard. Pack and serve.

VICTORIA PUNCH.

Boil three and one half cups water and two cups sugar fifteen minutes. Add the juice of four lemons and grated rind and juice of two oranges. Cool and partially freeze. Add one cup angelica, one cup cider, one and one half tablespoonfuls gin and freeze again. Alcoholic liquors retard freezing.

HOLLANDAISE PUNCH.

4 cups of water.	1 1/3 cups of sugar.
1/3 cup of lemon juice.	1 can pineapple.
1/4 cup of brandy.	2 tablespoonfuls of gin.

Cook the water, sugar, and a little grated lemon rind fifteen minutes. Add lemon juice and pineapple, cool, strain, and freeze partly, then add the liquor and continue freezing.

MONTROSE PUDDING.

1 cup of cream.	Yelks of 6 eggs.
1 cup of granulated sugar.	Vanilla.

Put a pint of cream on in a double boiler, and when hot add eggs and sugar. Cook until it thickens. Remove from the fire, add vanilla, and when cold, add one *pint of cream whipped.* When partially frozen line a mold and fill the center with raspberry, pineapple, or orange sherbet.

SAUCE.

1 tablespoon of gelatine.	Yelks of 3 eggs.
1/4 cup of powdered sugar.	1 tablespoon of vanilla.
1 pint of cream.	2 tablespoons brandy and sherry wine.

Dissolve the gelatine in a little hot water. Add the yelks of the eggs; add the sugar and the cream. Boil to a syrup. When it begins to thicken add the gelatine; remove from fire, and when cold add the vanilla, brandy, and sherry wine.

ORANGE ICE.

To four cups of sugar add a quart of water, and boil to a thick syrup. Add to this the juice of twelve oranges

and four lemons, and one quart of cold water. Put in a freezer and freeze. Pineapple or any water ice may be made in the same way.

FRUIT PUNCH.

Take the same syrup as above; add one quart of sherry, one half pint of brandy, one half pint of rum, one pound of candied cherries, one half pound candied pineapple, half a pound of grapes, and the juice of six lemons with the extra quart of cold water.

FRUIT ICE CREAM.

One half gallon fresh chopped peaches or fresh strawberries, sweetened to taste. Let stand in sugar over night or for several hours. Add one half gallon sweet cream and freeze.

FRUIT SAUCE.

One cup of sugar, one half cup of water boiled to a syrup, add fruit juice and boil until thick. If desired, add one half cup of whipped cream and serve cold, on cream or sherbet.

CHOCOLATE SAUCE.

1 cup of boiling water.   6 tablespoons of grated chocolate.
1/2 cup of sugar.   1/2 cup of milk.
1/2 tablespoon of arrowroot.

Boil the water and sugar; add the chocolate moistened with one half cup of milk, and the arrowroot dissolved in one half cup of water; boil three minutes. Strain and serve hot or cold, on ice cream or cake.

Grape juice is delicious served over sherbet.

NUT CARAMEL SAUCE FOR ICE CREAM.

One cup of maple syrup, one cup of sugar boiled until thick. Add one half cup of nut kernels chopped fine, or if more nuts are desired, add whole cup.

BRANDY SAUCE FOR ICE CREAM.

One cup of sugar and one cup of water boiled until thick. When cold add three tablespoons of brandy, or more if desired, and add one cup of whipped cream.

MISCELLANEOUS.

––––––––

COFFEE.

One cup of coffee (ground), one egg, one cup of cold water, six cups of boiling water. Scald coffee pot. Beat egg slightly, dilute with one half the cold water, add crushed shell and mix with coffee. Turn into coffee pot and pour on boiling water, and stir thoroughly. Place on front of range and boil three minutes. If not boiled, coffee is cloudy. If boiled too long, too much tannic acid is developed. Stir and pour some in a cup to be sure spout is free from grounds. Return to coffee pot and repeat. Add remaining cold water, which perfects clearing. Cold water being heavier than hot, sinks to the bottom, carrying grounds with it. Place on back of range for ten minutes where it will not boil. Serve at once.

PASTRY CRULLERS.

1 quart flour.	2 cups water.
2 eggs.	1 tablespoonful of butter.

Mix the flour and water, then the butter, then the beaten eggs and a little salt. Have the cruller iron heated thoroughly in boiling lard. Be very careful to drain all the lard from the iron, dip into some of the batter which you have put into a pint cup, being careful not to let the iron touch the bottom or sides of the cup; then dip in boiling lard and fry to a nice brown; remove from the iron and heat it again. Serve plain this way as a garnish, or sprinkle with cinnamon sugar as a cruller.

CHOCOLATE.

1 1/2 squares Baker's chocolate.	Few grains salt.
4 tablespoons sugar.	1 cup boiling water.
3 cups milk and cream.	

Scald milk and cream. Melt chocolate in small saucepan placed over hot water, add sugar, salt, and gradually boiling water; when smooth, place on range and boil one minute ; add to scalded milk and cream ; mill, and serve in chocolate cups with whipped cream. One and one half ounces vanilla chocolate may be substituted for Baker's chocolate; being sweetened, less sugar is required.

QUEEN FRITTERS.

One quarter (scant) cup of butter, one half cup of boiling water, one half cup of flour, two eggs. Put butter in small saucepan, and pour on water. As soon as the water reaches boiling point add flour all at once, and stir until mixture leaves sides of saucepan. Remove from fire and add eggs unbeaten, one at a time, beating mixture thoroughly between eggs. Drop by spoonfuls and fry in deep fat until well browned. Drain, make an opening and fill with preserves or fresh fruits. Sprinkle with sugar.

APPLE FRITTERS.

1 cup of flour.	2/3 cup of water.
1 tablespoon sugar.	1/2 tablespoon olive oil or
1/4 teaspoon salt.	Snowflake oil.
White of 1 egg.	2 medium sized sour apples.

Mix flour, sugar, and salt, add water gradually; then oil and white of egg beaten until stiff. Peel, core, and cut apples in eighths; then cut eighths in slices and stir into batter. Drop by spoonfuls and fry in deep fat. Drain on brown paper and sprinkle with powdered sugar. Serve hot.

SWEDISH TIMBALS.

One pint of flour, less two tablespoonfuls, one half pint sweet milk, three eggs, two tablespoonfuls olive oil or Snowflake oil, one teaspoonful of salt. Stir flour and milk to perfectly smooth batter, add oil, then salt and eggs. Dip timbal iron in boiling oil, then in batter, and then in fat, fill with fricasseed oysters with mushrooms.

OMELET.

Experience has taught us that an omelet is the most difficult to prepare of all egg dishes. In the first place an omelet pan should never be used for anything else. Before using, it is well to rub it with dry salt, to be sure it is perfectly smooth; and it is better to make several small omelets than to try to make one large one. Break from three to five eggs into a bowl, and beat twelve beats; sprinkle with salt and pepper and a few pieces of butter. Have the omelet pan hot, and put in just enough butter to cover the surface without being too greasy. Pour in the egg, and when it begins to cook, carefully cut it in several places so that the uncooked egg may cook evenly. Then take a broad knife and fold it over, placing the dish on which the omelet is to be served on top the omelet pan; lift the pan carefully and turn out on to the dish. Garnish with parsley.

CREAM CHICKEN.

1/2 boiled chicken.	1 pint of cream.
1 tablespoon of butter.	1/2 cup green peppers.
1 tablespoon of flour.	Salt, pepper, and celery.

Sauce to taste.

Melt one tablespoon of butter, add one tablespoon of flour, and when thoroughly blended add the cream and seasonings. Cook until thick, and add one half chicken which has been put through a meat grinder and one half cup of green peppers which have been parboiled and cut fine. Serve on buttered toast or patty shell.

EGG NOG.

12 eggs.	12 tablespoonfuls of sugar.
12 tablespoonfuls best whisky.	12 tablespoonfuls Jamaica rum.

Beat the yelks and sugar together until very light; then add the liquor slowly, next the whites, beaten to a stiff froth, and then one pint and a half of cream, whipped.

CHEESE RAMEQUINES.

Mix one half cup of grated cheese (mild), one tablespoon flour, one half saltspoon of salt, and a little cayenne pepper; add the well-beaten whites of three eggs. Shape in balls, allowing three tablespoonfuls for each ball, and fry in hot fat.

SALTED ALMONDS.

Blanch the almonds, wipe dry, place in a frying-basket, then into Snowflake oil] heated to the boiling point. When nicely browned, remove from the oil, sprinkle salt on them, and let them drain. Any other nut can be cooked in the same way.

FRUIT SALAD.

Equal quantities of green grapes, oranges, pineapples, grape fruit, maraschino, or candied cherries all cut up together and serve with sherry. This is delicious frozen and used as first course. The grapes and pineapples sweetened and frozen together with plenty of sherry make a delicious first course also.

A DAINTY FIRST COURSE.

Fill tall glass half full of maraschino or creme de menthe cherries. Put lemon or pineapple sherbet on top. Garnish with fresh mint.

ANCHOVY EGGS.

Cut hard-boiled eggs in two, lengthwise. (Boil the eggs twenty-five minutes, so that the yelks will be thoroughly done). Take out the yelks. Mash them well, mix them with mayonnaise dressing and the trimmings of the anchovies. Fill the one half with the mixture, covering the whole top. Trim anchovies to the right length and lay two of them across the top of each. To make it stand firm, slice a little piece from the bottom of the egg. Garnish with parsley and serve as first course.

MOLASSES TAFFY.

2 cups of brown sugar.	1 tablespoon butter.
3/4 cup of molasses.	2 teaspoons of vanilla.
	1/4 cup water.

Boil the sugar, molasses, and water until when dropped in a little cold water you can pick it up in your fingers. Then add butter and cook until candy is brittle when trying it in the water. Add the vanilla. Pour on buttered pans and pull. Be careful not to stir, or it will turn to sugar. When first put on to boil, a bit of cream of tartar will add to the lightness of it.

ICE CREAM CANDY.

2 cups of granulated or powdered sugar.	2 tablespoons of vinegar.
	1 tablespoon of butter.
1 cup of water.	2 tablespoons of vanilla.

Cook the same as molasses candy.

CHEESE CROQUETTES.

Grate half a pound of American cheese. Mix in it a scant tablespoonful of butter, a tablespoonful of milk, an egg beaten enough to break it, half a teaspoonful of salt, and a dash of paprika. Mix to a smooth paste and mold into small croquettes, using a tablespoonful of the paste for each croquette. The above proportions will make eight croquettes.

Add a little milk to the yelk of an egg and roll the croquettes in this and then in cracker dust. Then fry them for a minute in smoking hot fat. They should have a delicate brown color and be soft inside. Serve them as soon as they are fried, or the cheese will harden.

This is a delicious cheese dish and very easily made.

CHILI CONCARNI.

2 cans of tomatoes.	1 lemon minus the juice.
1 stalk of celery.	1 tablespoon of whole cloves.
9 red pepper pods.	tablespoon of whole allspice.

5 dried onions.   quarts of water.
3 pods of garlic.

Boil hard for two hours. Strain through colander. Put on at the same time two pounds of Hamburg steak in a little water; boil for two hours; add to this three cans of kidney beans. Add these to the tomatoes. Then add two tablespoons of Chili powder and serve hot. Enough for two meals for family of six.

CARAMELS.

1 1/2 pounds of brown sugar. 1/2 pound 1/4 pound of Baker's chocolate.
   of butter.   1 cup of cream or milk.

Put in kettle and boil until, when tried in cold water, a firm ball may be held in the fingers.

NUT CARAMELS.

1 cup of chocolate.   1 1/2 pounds of almonds blanched
1 pound of meat of English walnuts.   and chopped.

BUTTER SCOTCH.

1 cup of sugar.   1 tablespoon vinegar.
1/4 cup of molasses.   2 tablespoons of boiling water.
              1/2 cup of butter.

Boil the ingredients until, when tried in cold water, the mixture will be brittle. Flavor with vanilla. Pour into a well-buttered pan, and when cool, cut in squares.

RAISIN PICKLES.

2 pounds of raisins.   2 teaspoons white mustard.
3 dozen cucumbers (sliced).   2 teaspoons of celery.
Piece of stick cinnamon.   1 teaspoon black pepper.
3 teaspoons mace.   3 coffee cups brown sugar.
           1 quart of vinegar.

Put on the vinegar, spices, and sugar, and when it boils put in the raisins and let boil until clear. Pour all over the cucumbers which are ready in a vessel large enough to mix all together. If fresh cucumbers are used, soak in salt water over night. If pickled cucumbers are used, chop and add.

CUCUMBER PICKLE.

4 dozen cucumbers.	4 dozen onions.	24 green peppers.

Cut each cucumber in four pieces, scoop out the seeds and chop cucumber. Slice the onions and chop up the green peppers. Put all together in a bag. Put over them one quart of salt, tablespoon of celery seed, tablespoon allspice, one half tablespoon cloves and let stand over night. The same day take five quarts of vinegar made very sweet with sugar. Boil and let it stand over night. The next morning take the pickles out of the bag and put in jar. Pour over the five quarts of vinegar, and they are ready for use. This is delicious served with game or fish. Very pretty served in a half lemon scooped out.

SPANISH PICKLE.

2 dozen cucumbers large, or 4 dozen small.	1/2 dozen large green peppers.
1/2 peck of green tomatoes.	2 dozen white onions sliced.
	1/2 peck green beans.
1 cup of sugar.	

Cut the cucumbers in slices one inch thick, slice tomatoes thin and sprinkle with salt and let stand twenty-four hours. Then rinse off the salt. Grate two roots of horseradish, add one fourth pound of white mustard seed and five red peppers cut up. One ounce stick cinnamon. Make a paste of one pound of mustard, one ounce of celery seed, one ounce of turmeric, one pint Snowflake or olive oil.

Put vegetables in a pan and mix spices and paste all through them, scald enough vinegar (one gallon or more) to cover them. Pour over boiling hot. Stir every day or two. Ready for use in about two weeks. Makes three gallons.

GRAPE PICKLE.

7 pounds of grapes.	1 pint of vinegar.
3 1/2 pounds of sugar.	1 ounce of cloves.
1 ounce ground cinnamon.	

Pulp the grapes and boil until the seeds can be strained out through a sieve; then put the skins and all into the syrup and boil fifteen minutes or longer. Tie spices in a bag.

GREEN TOMATO PICKLE.

Slice a peck of small green tomatoes thin and half as many nice onions. Place them in layers in a stone jar. Sprinkle each layer very lightly with salt. Weight them down for twelve hours, then let them drain (I put mine in separate jars or bags). Put in a porcelain kettle, sprinkle through them one half pound white mustard seed. In a bowl put

2 pounds of sugar.	1 heaping tablespoon cinnamon.
1 teaspoon mace (heaping).	1 heaping tablespoon ginger.
1 teaspoon allspice.	heaping tablespoon black pepper.
1 teaspoon cloves.	tablespoons of celery seed.

Mix all of these ingredients with a little cold vinegar until smooth, then add a gallon more. Turn over the tomatoes with some strips of horseradish; stew slowly and stir often with a wooden spoon to prevent burning. Ready for use as soon as cold. This is good either sliced or chopped.

BANANA CROQUETTES.

Remove the skin and coarse threads from the banana and trim pulp of each to a long croquette. Roll in an egg beaten with a teaspoonful of cold water and then in bread crumbs seasoned with salt and pepper. Fry one half minute in hot fat. Drain on soft paper.

BRANDY PEACHES.

Peel and weigh the peaches and put to them about half the weight of sugar. Put in the kettle just enough water to moisten the sugar and let boil until the peaches are done enough to pierce to the seed with a straw. Then take them out and put on dishes. Boil syrup until it is quite thick. Then put in a bowl to cool. To three pints of syrup add two pints of whisky or brandy, and pour it over the peaches in air-tight jars.

EGGS BAKED IN TOMATOES.

Select round tomatoes of uniform size. Cut off the stem ends and take out enough of the pulp to leave a space as large as an egg. Sprinkle the inside with salt and pepper. Drop into each one an egg. Place the filled tomatoes in a baking-dish with a little hot water, and bake them about fifteen minutes, or until the eggs are set and the tomatoes are a little softened. Serve the eggs on rounds of bread browned in butter. No sauce is required with this dish.

BOILED HAM.

Soak several hours or over night in cold water to cover. Wash thoroughly, trim off hard skin near end of bone, put in a kettle, cover with cold water, heat to boiling point, and cook slowly until tender. Remove kettle from range and set aside, that ham may partially cool; then take from water, remove outside skin, sprinkle with sugar and fine cracker crumbs, and stick with cloves one half inch apart. Bake one hour in a slow oven. Serve cold, thinly sliced. Boil four to five hours.

OATMEAL WITH SLICED BANANAS.

Have the water salty—one half teaspoon to a pint of freshly boiled water. Stir in slowly one cup of steam- cooked oats to two cups of water. Let boil up once after all the grain is added. Then set into hot water kettle or double boiler and cook from one half hour to a full hour; the latter is preferable. Pour into patent charlotte russe molds or cups and let it stand over night. In the morning turn from the molds into a hot baking sheet and set in the oven until very hot. If molded in cups remove the centers, leaving a wall of the oatmeal. Remove to the serving dishes with a broad-bladed knife and fill the centers with slices of banana. Put a spoonful of whipped cream above the bananas, and serve in a nest of whipped cream.

HOW TO MAKE TEA.

3 teaspoons tea.   2 cups boiling water.

Scald an earthen or china teapot. Put in tea, and pour on boiling water. Let stand on back of range or in a warm place five minutes. Strain and serve immediately, with or without sugar and milk. Avoid second steeping of leaves with addition of a few fresh ones. If this is done, so large an amount of tannin is extracted that various ills are apt to follow.

RUSSIAN TEA.

Follow recipe for making tea. Russian tea may be served hot or cold, but always without milk. A thin slice of lemon, from which seeds have been removed, or a few drops of lemon juice, is allowed for each cup. Sugar is added according to taste. In Russia a preserved strawberry to each cup is considered an improvement. We imitate our Russian friends by garnishing with a candied cherry.

SIMPLE DISHES FOR THE SICK.

TOAST WATER.

Toast three slices of stale bread to a dark brown, but do not burn. Put into a pitcher, pour over them one quart boiling water. Cover closely and let stand on ice until cold. Strain. If desired, wine and sugar may be added.

RICE WATER.

Pick over and wash two tablespoonfuls of rice. Put into a granite saucepan with one quart boiling water. Simmer two hours, when rice should be softened and partially dissolved. Strain; add a saltspoonful of salt. Serve warm or cold. Two tablespoonfuls of sherry or port may be added if desired.

BARLEY WATER.

Wash two ounces (one wineglassful) of pearl barley with cold water. Boil five minutes in fresh water. Throw both waters away; pour on two quarts of boiling water and boil down to one quart. Flavor with thinly cut lemon rind. Add sugar to taste. Do not strain unless at the patient's request.

EGG WATER.

Stir the whites of two eggs into half a pint of ice water without beating the eggs. Add enough salt or sugar to make palatable.

FLAXSEED TEA.

Flaxseed, whole, 1 ounce (1 heaping tablespoonful). White sugar, 1 ounce.
Lemon juice, 4 tablespoonfuls.
Licorice root, 1/2 ounce (two small sticks).

99

Pour on these materials two pints of boiling water. Let stand in a hot place four hours and strain off the liquor.

PEPTONIZED MILK (Cold Process).

In a clean quart bottle put one peptonizing powder (extract of pancreas 5 grains, bicarbonate of soda 15 grains — or the contents of one peptonizing tube—Fairchild), add one teacup of cold water and shake well. Add one pint of fresh cold milk and shake mixture again. Place on ice. Use when required without subjecting to heat.

PEPTONIZED MILK (Warm Process).

Mix peptonizing powder with water and milk as described above; place bottle in water only so hot that the whole hand can be held in it a minute without discomfort. Keep the bottle there ten minutes. Then put on ice to check further digestion. Do not heat long enough to render the milk bitter.

PEPTONIZED MILK TOAST.

Over two slices of toast pour one gill of peptonized milk (cold process), let stand on the back of stove thirty minutes, serve warm or strain and serve fluid portion alone. Plain, light sponge cake may be similarly digested.

KOUMISS.

Take ordinary beer bottle with shifting cork, put in it one pint of milk, one sixth of a cake of Fleischmann's yeast, or one tablespoonful of fresh lager beer yeast (brewer's), one half of a tablespoonful of white sugar reduced to a syrup. Shake well and allow it to stand in the refrigerator two or three days, when it may be used. It will keep there indefinitely if laid on its side. Much waste can be saved by preparing the bottles with ordinary corks wired in position, and drawing off the koumiss with a champagne tap.

CREAMED OATMEAL.

Boil oatmeal as for breakfast, rub it through a fine sieve, add a little cream, and cook very slowly in a double boiler for half an hour longer. When perfectly smooth, add a very little salt and rich cream. This is the most delicate preparation of oatmeal that an invalid can take.

CREAMED SWEETBREADS.

Make sauce as for creamed chicken (on page 116). Add parboiled sweetbreads chopped fine and a tablespoonful of sherry wine.

PANNED OYSTERS.

Put two tablespoonfuls of butter in a saute pan. Lay twenty good-sized oysters into it. When the edges curl and the oysters plump, dust them with pepper and salt, and serve at once on toast. Two tablespoonfuls of sherry can be added before serving if desired.

RAW MEAT DIET.

Scrape pulp from a good steak; season to taste. Spread on slices of bread, then sear the bread slightly, and serve as a sandwich.

APPLE SOUP.

Two cups of raw apple, two cups of water, two teaspoonfuls of com starch, one and a half tablespoonfuls of sugar, one saltspoonful of cinnamon, and a bit of salt. Stew the apple in the water until it is very soft. Then mix together in a smooth paste the corn starch, sugar, salt, and cinnamon with a little cold water. Pour this into the apple and boil five minutes. Strain it and keep hot until ready to serve. May serve with cream if desired.

BEEF MINCE.

Have a pound of beef from the round. Free it from all sinews and fat. Mince it very fine. To two tablespoonfuls of butter in a saucepan put in the meat and a teaspoonful of onion juice. Stir for three or four minutes, or until the meat is hot through. Add salt and pepper, and if desired a little lemon juice. Serve on hot buttered toast.

FLAXSEED LEMONADE.

One tablespoonful of whole flaxseed, one pint of boiling water, lemon juice, and sugar. Pick over and wash the flaxseed, add water, and cook two hours, keeping just below the boiling point. Strain; add lemon juice and sugar to taste.

ORANGEADE.

Juice of 1 orange.   1 1/2 tablespoonfuls of syrup.
2 tablespoonfuls of crushed ice.

Make a syrup by boiling eight minutes one cup of water and half a cup of sugar. Mix the orange juice and the syrup, and pour over the crushed ice.

SHERRY NOG.

To the yelk of one egg thoroughly beaten add one tablespoonful of powdered sugar and two tablespoonfuls of sherry wine and a pint of whipped cream.

MILK PUNCH.

1/2 cup milk.   Sugar.
1 tablespoon whisky, rum, or brandy. Few gratings nutmeg.

Mix ingredients, cover, and shake well.

COCOA CORDIAL.

1 teaspoon cocoa.   1/2 cup boiling water.
1 teaspoon sugar.   1 1/2 tablespoons port wine.

Mix cocoa and sugar, add enough of the water to form a paste. Stir in remainder of water and boil one minute, then add wine. Useful in cases of chill or exhaustion.

PEPTONIZED OYSTERS.

Mince six large or twelve small oysters. Add to them, in their own liquor, five grains extract of pancreas with fifteen grains bicarbonate of soda, or one Fairchild peptonizing tube. The mixture is then brought to a blood heat and maintained, with occasional stirring, at that temperature thirty minutes, when one pint of milk is added and the temperature kept up ten to twenty minutes. Finally the mass is brought to a boiling point; strain and serve. Gelatine may be added and the mixture served cold as a jelly. Cooked tomatoes, onions, celery, or other flavoring suited to individual tastes may be added at the beginning of artificial digestion.

BEEF TEA.

Free a pound of lean beef from fat, tendon, cartilage, bone, and vessels; chop up fine, put into a pint of cold water for two hours. Simmer on the stove three hours, but do not boil. Make up for the water lost by adding cold water so that a pint of beef tea represents one pound of beef. Press the beef very carefully, and strain.

BEEF JUICE.

Cut a thin, juicy steak into pieces about one and one half inches square. Sear separately one and one half minutes, on each side, over a hot fire. Squeeze in a hot lemon squeezer, flavor with salt and pepper. May add to milk, or pour on toast.

MEAT CURE.

Procure slices of steak from the top of the round, without fat. Cut meat into strips, removing all fat, gristle, etc., with a knife. Put meat through mincer at least twice. Then beat it well in a roomy saucepan with cold water or skimmed beef tea, to the consistency of cream. The right proportion is one teaspoonful of liquid to eight of pulp. Add black pepper and salt to taste. Stir the mince briskly with a wooden spoon the whole time it is cooking, over a slow fire, or on the cool part of cupboard range, until hot through and through and the red color disappears. This requires one and one half hours. When done it should be a soft, stiff, smooth puree, of the consistency of good paste. Serve hot. Add for the first few meals a softly poached white of an egg.

STERILIZED MILK.

Put the required amount of milk in clean bottles; if for infants, each bottle holding enough for one feeding. Plug the mouths lightly with rubber stoppers, immerse to the shoulders in a kettle of cold water. Boil twenty minutes, or better, steam thirty minutes in ordinary steamer. Push in the stoppers firmly, cool the bottles rapidly, and keep in a refrigerator. Warm each bottle just before using.

BEEF TEA WITH ACID.

One and one half pounds of beef from the round, cut in small pieces; same quantity ice broken small. Let it stand in a deep vessel twelve hours; strain thoroughly and forcibly through a coarse towel. Boil quickly ten minutes in a porcelain vessel. Let cool. Add one half teaspoonful of acid, or acid phosphate, to a pint. Serve hot or cold.

OATMEAL GRUEL.

One half a cup of coarse oatmeal, three cups boiling water, one teaspoonful of salt, and cream. Add oatmeal and salt to boiling water, and cook three hours in a double boiler. Force through a strainer, dilute with cream, reheat and strain a second time. Serve with salt or sugar.

CREAMED EGGS.

1/3 glassful of chicken stock.	4 eggs.
1/3 glassful of cream.	1/2 teaspoonful of salt.
	Pepper to taste.

Heat together the cream and the stock in a double boiler. Beat the eggs without separating, and stir into it slowly. Stir until thick, season and serve. This is the most nourishing preparation of eggs for an invalid.

CREAMED CALF BRAINS.

Parboil the brains. Blanch them and cut into small pieces. Put into a double boiler one tablespoonful of butter and a scant one of flour. Add half a pint of cream. Put in slowly the beaten yelk of one egg, stirring constantly. Season with salt and pepper, add the brains, cook three minutes, and serve on toast.

CREAMED CHICKEN.

One tablespoonful of butter and one of flour, and add to that half a pint of cream, a little salt, pepper, and celery salt and the meat from half a chicken which has been put through the meat grinder.

MUTTON BROTH.

Lean loin of mutton, one and one half pounds, including bone. Three pints of water. Boil gently until tender, throwing in a little salt and onion, according to taste. Pour out broth into basin; when cold, skim off the fat. Warm up when wanted.

CHICKEN BROTH.

Chop up a small chicken, or half of a large fowl. Boil it, bones and all, with a blade of mace, a sprig of parsley, a tablespoonful of rice, and a crust of bread in one quart of water, for an hour, skimming it from time to time. Strain through a colander.

EGG LEMONADE.

Beat one egg with one tablespoonful of sugar until very light; stir in three tablespoonfuls cold water and the juice of a small lemon. Fill the glass with pounded ice and drink through a straw.

CREAM SOUP.

Take one quart of good stock, chicken or mutton; cut one onion into quarters, slice three potatoes very thin and put into the stock with a small piece of mace. Boil gently for an hour. Then strain out the onion and mace. The potatoes should by this time have dissolved in the stock. Add one pint of milk, a very little corn flour to make it about as thick as cream, and a little butter. This soup may be made with milk instead of stock, if a little cream is used with it.

WINE WHEY.

Put two pints of new milk in a saucepan and stir over a clear fire until nearly boiling. Then add one gill (two wineglassfuls) of sherry and simmer a quarter of an hour, skimming off the curd as it rises. Add one tablespoonful more of sherry and skim again for a few minutes. Strain through coarse muslin. May use two tablespoonfuls of lemon juice instead of wine if desired.

JUNKET.

Take one half pint of fresh milk, heated lukewarm. Add one teaspoonful essence of pepsin and stir just enough to mix. Pour into custard cups and let it stand until firmly curded. Serve plain or with sugar and grated nutmeg. May add sherry.

RUM PUNCH.

White sugar two teaspoonfuls, one egg beaten up. Add a large wineglassful warm milk, two to four teaspoonfuls Jamaica rum, and a little nutmeg.

MILK AND EGGS.

Beat milk with salt to taste. Beat white of egg until stiff. Add egg to milk and stir.

CHAMPAGNE WHEY.

Boil one half pint of milk. Strain through cheesecloth and add one wineglass of champagne.

DAINTY MENUS

FOR CONVALESCENT PATIENTS.

Select the daintiest of tray covers and china, and make the tray look as attractive as possible in every way.

No. 1.

Bouillon.

Creamed Chicken on Toast.

garnished with parsley.

Bread and Butter Sandwiches, served on lettuce leaf.

Small Mold Bavarian Cream with whipped cream.

No. 2.

Cream of Celery Soup.

Supreme of Chicken with White Sauce, garnished with

parsley.

Beaten Biscuit.

One Fresh Tomato, garnished with chopped celery or

Nasturtium leaves.

Mold of Wine Jelly.

No. 3.

Broiled Breast of Chicken with drawn butter.

Creamed Sweetbreads on Toast with peas.

Bread and Butter Sandwiches.

Cup of Delicate Chocolate.

A Little Whipped Cream, frozen.

No. 4.

An Orange cut in half, after being on ice several hours.

Broiled Sweetbread, garnished.

Quail on Toast.

Celery Salad, garnished with celery tops.

Bread Sticks.

Pineapple Ice.

No. 5.

Oyster Soup.

Fish Coquille in a nest of water cress or parsley.

Broiled Beef Tenderloin, mushroom sauce.

Parisienne Potatoes.

Light Rolls.

Brandy Peaches.

No. 6.

Sweetbread Croquettes with creamed peas.

Bread and Butter Sandwiches.

Celery Salad.

Chocolate with whipped cream.

Plain Ice Cream.

No. 7.

Shredded wheat biscuit toasted and served with

hot milk or cream.

(Serve in dainty pitcher.)

Crisp Breakfast Bacon in parsley.

Poached Egg on toast.

Breakfast Cocoa.

No. 8.

Fresh Pineapple plugged, sugared; cover in crushed

ice, and garnish with mint leaves.

Broiled Breast of Chicken with drawn butter.

Fresh Tomato (thoroughly chilled) garnished with

water cress; serve with or without dressing.

Strawberry Sponge.

CHAPTER ON MENUS.

SIMPLE LUNCHEON.

No. 1.

Sliced Pineapple with crushed ice and sherry.

Bouillon.

Oyster Patties.

Stuffed Lamb Chops with peas.

Egg Salad.

Brick Cream and Cakes.

Coffee.

No. 2.

Puree of Asparagus with whipped cream garnish.

Oysters en Coquille.

Chicken Croquettes with creamed peas.

Celery Salad.

Bavarian Cream. Macaroons.

Coffee.

No. 3.

Tomato Puree.

Mushrooms a l'Algonquin on Toast.

Broiled Fillets. Potatoes en Surprise.

Hollandaise Punch.

Pepper Timbals.

Chicken Salad.

Individual Orange Ice with Cakes.

Coffee.

No. 4.

Grape Fruit.

Bouillon.

Fish Croquettes with white sauce. Potatoes.

Broiled Quail on Toast with asparagus.

Hollandaise Punch.

Little Pigs in Blankets (Sweetbreads).

Waldorf Salad.

Individual Ices and Cakes.

Coffee.

No. 5.

Large Pink Grapes served in crushed ice with sherry wine.

Lobster Cutlets with bechamel sauce.

Broiled Grouse. Potatoes en Surprise with oyster sauce.

Victoria Punch.

Croquettes of French Peas with sauce.

Salad a la Jardin.

Individual Brick. Cake.

Coffee.

No. 6.

Oyster Bisque.

Fish Croquettes with Potatoes.

Broiled Quail. Saratoga Chips. Asparagus.

Punch.

Supreme of Chicken with bechamel sauce.

Green Grape Salad.

Ice Cream with Brandied Fruit. Cakes.

Coffee.

INFORMAL DINNER.

No. 1.

Salted Almonds. Olives.

Chicken Gumbo.

Fish Pudding. Parisienne Potatoes.

Roast Turkey, Cranberry Sauce. Croquettes of Peas.

Asparagus, and Stuffed Sweet Potatoes.

Celery Salad.

Charlotte Russe, or Ices.

Coffee.

No. 2.

Salted Almonds, Pickles, and Celery.

St. Germain Soup.

Broiled Pompano. Potatoes au Gratin.

Grouse or Pheasant. Asparagus. Peas.

Nut and Celery Salad.

Fig Pudding with fancy sauce.

No. 3.

Salted Pecans. Stuffed Olives.

Consomme. Croutons.

Baked Fish. Duchess Potatoes. Beaten Biscuit.

Roast Fillet of Beef. Brussels Sprouts. Stuffed Tomatoes. Rolls.

Cucumber and Celery Salad. Wafers.

Baked Caramel Custard. Cake. Coffee.

No. 4.

Salted Almonds. Mints.

Frozen Fruit.

Cream of Celery Soup. Bread Sticks.

Oyster Croquettes. French Fried Potatoes. Beaten Biscuit.

Broiled Quail or Broiled Chicken Breast with Mushrooms.

Asparagus Tips. Stuffed Sweet Potatoes. Rolls.

Green Grape and Nut Salad. Wafers.

Sultana Roll and Claret Sauce. Cake.

Coffee.

No. 5.

Salted Pecans. Mints.

Grape Fruit.

Cream of Pea Soup. Buttered Toast.

Salpicon of Lobster in Patty Shells.

Lamb Chops a la Maintenon. Parisienne Potatoes. Hot Rolls.

Sweet Bread, Cucumber and Celery Salad. Cheese Sticks.

Montrose Pudding with sauce. Cakes.

Coffee.

No. 6.

Salted Almonds. Mints.

Pineapple Sherbet—Creme de menthe Cherries.

Cream of Asparagus Soup. Crackers.

Soft Shell Crabs. Beaten Biscuit. Cucumbers.

Stuffed Peppers. Rolls. Peas.

Pineapple and Nut Salad. Cheese Wafers.

Nesselbrode Pudding. Cakes.

Coffee.

DINNER.

No. 1.

Salted Almonds. Maron Glace.

Blue Points on Half Shell.

Consomme.

Lobster Timbals with lobster sauce.

Fillet of Beef. Parisienne Potatoes. Asparagus.

Victoria Punch.

Stuffed Quail. Croquettes of Peas with white sauce.

Stuffed Mushrooms.

Celery Salad. Fancy Ices and Cakes.

Coffee.

No, 2.

Blue Points on Half Shell.

Consomme.

Stuffed Lobster.

Fillet of Beef. Creamed Cauliflower. Potatoes.

Roman Punch.

Broiled Grouse with Asparagus.

Sweetbread Croquettes

with peas.

Green Grape Salad.

Fancy Ices and Cakes.

Coffee.

No. 3.

Oyster Cocktail.

Cream of Celery Soup with whipped cream garnish.

Lobster a la Newburg.

Venison Steaks. Asparagus.

Roman Punch.

Sweetbread a la Victoria, allemande sauce. Peas.

Salad a la Jardin, in turnips.

Sultana Roll Ice with claret sauce. Cakes.

Coffee.

No. 4.

Caviare on Toast.

Consomme.

Lobster Timbals.

Fillet of Beef. Stuffed Sweet Potatoes. Asparagus.

Fruit Punch.

Pheasant. Potatoes en Surprise with sauce.

Stuffed Mushrooms.

Waldorf Salad.

Fancy Ices and Cake.

Coffee.

No. 5.

Salted Nuts. Mints.

Anchovy Eggs.

Oyster Bisque. Crackers.

Baked Fish. Potatoes. Cucumbers. Bread.

Stuffed Chicken Leg. Peas. Hot Rolls.

Victoria Punch.

Individual Fillet with Mushrooms.

Cauliflower au Gratin. Rolls.

Green Pepper and Grape Fruit Salad. Cheese Ramequins.

Brandy Peaches with Vanilla Cream. Cakes.

Coffee.

No. 6.

Fresh Strawberries with caps,

served on shaved ice, powdered sugar (served in paper cups).

Bouillon. Croutons.

Soft Shell Crabs or Lobster Cutlets. Cucumbers in cucumber

cups. Beaten Biscuit.

Chicken Livers en Brochette, sauce. Bread and Butter Sandwiches.

Hollandaise Punch.

Broiled Chicken. French Pea Croquettes. Broiled

Tomatoes. Hot Rolls.

Water Cress and Orange Salad. Cheese Sticks.

Individual Ices. Cakes.

Coffee.

MEMORANDA.

The following blank pages are intended for recording recipes that may hereafter come to notice, or for any data on those contained herein.

Housekeepers' Directory

121

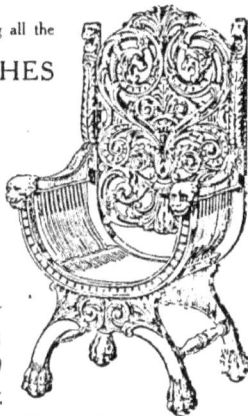

125

JENNIE C. BENEDICT

LOUISVILLE GAS COMPANY

Makes the cleanest, purest gas of uniform quality and low pressure, most suitable for

GAS RANGES

The Gas Range is the most useful invention of modern times for economical cooking.

"The Purest and Best"

CAMEO
BAKING POWDER

If your grocer does not keep it he can send to

THOMSON & TAYLOR,
MICHIGAN AVENUE,
CHICAGO